The Pillow Book of Eleanor Bron

'A pillow book was a various thing – a cross between a journal and a commonplace book, a place to note impressions and thoughts as well as events, anecdotes, complaints, pleasures, lists of anything that took the fancy – a general sifting of experience.'

After graduating from Cambridge in Modern Languages, the actress and writer Eleanor Bron first became known in the 1960s in satirical cabaret with *The Establishment* and on television. She went on to be equally admired as a dramatic actress, playing roles such as Yelena in *Uncle Vanya*, Amanda in *Private Lives*, Natasha in *A Month in the Country*, Hesione in *Heartbreak House*, as well as Jean Brodie, Hedda Gabler and Cleopatra. More recently she joined the McKellen/Petherbridge Company at the National Theatre to play the Duchess of Malfi in Philip Rowse's production, as well as Varya in *The Cherry Orchard* and Lady Cynthia Muldoon in *The Real Inspector Hound*. The films in which she has appeared range from *Help!*, *Bedazzled* and *Two for the Road*, to *Little Dorrit* and Ken Russell's *Women in Love*. On television she has appeared in the *Rumpole* series, *Dr Who* and *Yes, Minister*, in *Making Faces*, which was written for her by Michael Frayn; and with John Fortune she wrote and performed several series for television on which they based their book *Is Your Marriage Really Necessary?* Her other writing includes a song cycle about Mary, Queen of Scots and Elizabeth I; new verses to Saint Saens' *Carnival of the Animals*; and she has contributed both to the book of essays *My Cambridge* and to the BBC series *Words* and *Shakespeare in Perspective*. Before her *Pillow Book* she wrote another autobiographical book called *Life and Other Punctures*.

THE
PILLOW BOOK
OF
Eleanor Bron
OR
AN ACTRESS DESPAIRS

A METHUEN PAPERBACK

By the same Author

Is Your Marriage Really Necessary? (with John Fortune)
Life and Other Punctures

A METHUEN PAPERBACK
First published in 1985
by Jonathan Cape Ltd
32 Bedford Square, London WC1B 3EL
This paperback edition first published in 1987
by Methuen London Ltd
11 New Fetter Lane, London EC4P 4EE
Copyright © Eleanor Bron 1985

Printed and bound in Great Britain by
Richard Clay Ltd, Bungay, Suffolk

British Library Cataloguing in Publication Data

Bron, Eleanor
    The pillowbook of Eleanor Bron, or, An
    actress despairs.
    1. Bron, Eleanor   2. Actors—Great Britain
    —Biography
    I. Title
    792'.028'0924   PN2598.B68/

    ISBN 0-413-15070-4

to my Parents

The frontispiece illustration shows Eleanor Bron
in her *One Woman Show* and is reproduced
by courtesy of Liverpool Playhouse.

The author and publishers would like to thank
the following for permission to reproduce
copyright material: King's College, Cambridge, p. 46;
Albert Rustling, p. 57; Derek Balmer, p. 91.

The authors and publishers would also like to thank
Edward Petherbridge and Jennifer Beeston for permission
to reproduce photographic material on the cover
of the book.

Acknowledgements

and thanks go chiefly to Faith Evans for her persistence and resilience, and good cheer verging on saintliness; and to Howard Schuman for his insight, understanding, generosity and lavish time. Other friends also read – persevering with a difficult dot-matrix typescript – and enthused, criticised or went very quiet; in particular Cedric, Gavin, Richard Scott-Simon and Harriet Wasserman. The fact that I have so often ignored their useful advice does not mean that I am entirely heedless and ungrateful, or that it was wasted – since some of the advice was to ignore any advice.

More thanks to Eva Paneth for her eye on my German, and for reminding me of the pleasures of translation; to my brother Gerry and his family for allowing me at odd times to invade their privacy to tackle a computer terminal for my first essay at word-processing; to everyone at the Bron office for their friendliness and help as well as to Pat Carthy and Don Smith at BBC Publications; and to Valerie Buckingham and Jo Angell at Cape for patience and care beyond the call of duty.

Last, and almost foremost, I have belatedly to thank Arnold Freedman, who introduced me to Sei Shōnagon, so long ago.

Preface

A colleague of my brother has the happy ability to transmit his passionate enthusiasms to his friends, often in tangible form. Some sixteen years ago his current passion was a Japanese diary of one of the ladies-in-waiting to the Empress Sadako, written towards the end of the tenth century. He gave me a copy: *The Pillow Book of Sei Shōnagon*.

A pillow book was a various thing – a cross between a journal and a commonplace book, a place to note impressions and thoughts as well as events, anecdotes, pleasures, lists of anything that took the fancy – a general sifting of experience. (It was called a pillow book because its pages were sometimes kept in a drawer in one of the wooden pillows that look so comfortless to Western eyes – and the author would pen last thoughts and reflections before retiring.) Sei Shōnagon describes how she came into possession of a large quantity of paper and 'set about filling it with odd facts, stories from the past and all sorts of things, often including the most trivial material. On the whole I concentrated on things and people and observations on trees and plants, birds and insects. I was sure when people saw my book they would say "It's even worse than I expected. Now one can really tell what she is like."'

Even across the centuries and in spite of the total obscurity, for most modern readers, of the illustrious figures Sei Shōnagon sets before us, it is still very clear what she was like, and the world in which she lived; which is what struck me when I took her pillow book off the shelf again two years ago. Suddenly I saw in its now direct, now oblique form, a possible direction for a further instalment of autobiography. The randomness of the book attracted me, and its scope, and the fact that, in spite of the unusual opportunities it offers to distance and to abstract, it is peculiarly immediate and personal.

Since I was fifteen I have kept an intermittent journal, living always in terror lest my precious exercise books be discovered and my inmost secrets spilled before the gasping, prurient world. This obsessive youthful fear of betrayal led me in those journals into labyrinths of wilful obscurity which even I can no longer penetrate. Who on earth was it that I was on about on that long ago Sunday March 10; who was it then that was conjuring my passion, my pity, my reviling? (By contrast my essays into fiction, when I read them after only a few years' space, hold no secrets. My cunningly disguised characters leap off the page as living breathing highly recognisable, not to say actionable, friends and foes; even their assumed names shout Freudian clues at me.)

My pillow book is put together from the clues provided by these cryptic and spasmodic journals, from daily appointment diaries, from letters, from scrapbooks kept with care by my parents over the last twenty years, whenever I remembered to send them cuttings, and from memory variously jogged by these clues.

Nowadays I keep a journal because I am aware of how much of my life I shall lose to oblivion if I don't. I am not enough of a journalist to undertake a journey, or keep a diary, with publication in mind. To know that I was going to record the happenings of each day for that purpose would almost certainly distort the view for me. Not being a journalist, though, has meant that over the score of years that my notebooks cover, my main subject has been me: I used the pages as an outlet or even outpouring in time of need, when there was no other ear, or when all available ears had been mercilessly bent. So there is in these records a plangent imbalance – a tendency to record the woes and not the exultations. It is only relatively recently that this all-absorbing interest has begun to wane and I prefer to record externals and to look outward at least some of the time.

And over the years the need for secrecy has mellowed a little into a simple desire for privacy – a desire not compatible, in the view of many people, with working in the public eye as an actress.

I don't agree with that view but I can see that there are difficulties about writing any sort of autobiography and still hankering after some remnant of privacy. Privacy would be no problem at all if it were a self-contained thing. The difficulty is that one person's privacy may involve another's. What you reveal about yourself is your own affair but if you reveal your own affairs, of whatever nature, you are likely to be encroaching on someone else's life. In the context of work such revelation seems an unethical act; in the context of friendship, unforgivably rude. So – and for this my friends may not thank me, and my colleagues may well curse me – I have from time to time changed their names; and it seemed nice to be able to simplify life for once in a way by ubiquitously dubbing any requited Tom, Dick or Harry who happens to stray onto these pages, with the universally popular name of John. To avoid, or occasionally abet, confusion, I have where necessary distinguished the real, and often distinguished Johns from the merely beloved, by adding their surnames.

My career as an actress, which is roughly spanned by what follows, has not been an especially typical one. I went to University and not to Drama School and although there were many more true repertory theatres active then I spent only a single belated season with one of these companies, at Bristol, and did not serve any theatrical apprenticeship to my career. This was because I happened to become an actress at the time – in the early 1960s – of the 'Satire Boom', and was flung into household-namedom by appearing three nights a week live on the television series 'Not So Much a Programme More a Way of Life' which was the successor to 'That Was the Week That Was'. My first professional job was with 'The Establishment', called 'London's First Satirical Nightclub', which Peter Cook opened, with Nick Luard, in his time off from 'Beyond the Fringe'. I had no Equity card – mandatory today – and was lucky to get into the profession at all. The cast of 'The Establishment' did the T.V. pilot for TW3 and then left the country, for the Promised Land of Satire, the United States, home of Mort

Sahl and Lenny Bruce. Back in England, after an exhilarating year or two, the satirical tag, coupled with the odium which a university degree can hang on a girl, was beginning to throttle me. Such regard as I had for my own facility, for accents and lightning character changes, quickly evaporated when it began to seem a barrier rather than a password. People love you to make them laugh. They will forgive dramatic actors who try their hand at comedy, but they feel cheated if it happens the other way about; and satire, with its dangerous suggestion of social and political awareness, and threat of cleverness, is even more of a straightjacket than simple comedy. I had the impression that comedy was assumed by many to be something that got stuck on from the outside whereas tragedy and drama were to be painfully dredged from the gut, but I found this hard to accept. From any point of view, of approach, of method, of technique, I thought it an arbitrary distinction. The same sources and resources – observation, memory, intelligence, intuition, emotion, etc. – are necessary to both. If there has to be a dividing line between comedy and tragedy the closer you can play to the net, the better. From those early days to today my diaries and scrapbooks reflect my sometimes convoluted struggles to earn both a living and the right to be called not a satirist or a funny lady or even a dramatic actress, but just – a good actress.

Time has removed Sei Shōnagon's pillow book beyond person-alities, though her own emerges so vividly. A thousand years later we glimpse what it was like to be a lady-in-waiting in her day, as well as what it was like to be her. It would be fanciful to try to draw parallels between a Japanese lady-in-waiting and an English actress today – although lady-in-waiting is a description that fits too many of the actor sorority, myself included, too often. Even if you are violently successful in this business there are almost inevitably battles and disappointments. At any given moment over 75 to 80 per cent of all actors are out of work, and if you are a woman your chances for active involvement in even the painful aspects of the work are still fewer. Stanislavski's classic is called *An Actor Prepares* but an actress all too often has nothing to prepare for. As in politics, and so many other fields, talent is not always a guarantee of work; failure is not always related to ability; success is not always an indication of artistic worth. But I hope that the ups and downs of what follows – in roughly chronological order – may give you an idea of what it is like to be any actress, as well as what it is like to be me.

When she is carried away she is sincere, like all passionate women. Pride also sometimes prevents her from lying.

Ivan Turgenev, *Smoke*

THE
PILLOW BOOK
OF
Eleanor Bron

1 THE FIRST THING I SAW when I woke up after the first night was the sun pouring through the long balcony window and lighting up the flowers Peter had given me, thrust into a bucket until I had time to arrange them. But they looked so happy and glorious and profuse jostling all together there, that I decided to break their stems and put them back where they were, instead of separating and sorting and dotting them in groups, in an attempt at elegance.

2 TESSA CAME TO SEE THE SHOW LAST NIGHT; she remarked that it was nice for once not to be visiting each other in hospital – the last time she saw me I was flat out after my spinal fusion and the time before that I was visiting her in a discreet women's ward. She had been having an affair with a married man who promised to leave his wife, but kept putting it off 'because of the children'. When she found that she was pregnant he became very alarmed. He begged her to get rid of the child, which shocked Tessa profoundly – not because she was religious, but because he was. She refused to have an abortion, which was illegal and difficult and sordid. He used her refusal as an excuse to break with her, saying that they had both gone into the affair with their eyes open – he was not to be blamed if she was unreasonable; he had thought she was a modern, reasonable girl. She never saw him again – though when his marriage broke up five years later he did try to see her and his son – but when the baby was born she sent a telegram to his home with the message, 'Congratulations – it's a bastard, like you.'

1

3. I WAS STRUCK BY THE IRONY of the fact that our first show at the Establishment begins at 9 p.m. which, for five months, had been 'Lights Out' in the hospital ward, often followed by a dreary long night; or I would wake up at four and be unable to get back to sleep. Now, after finishing the second show and perhaps having a drink, I am just on my way back home at four a.m., and ready for my bed, as indeed is John.

4   *endearing things*

— my grandfather drinking his tea with a noisy smacking of his lips after each sip, to show his appreciation

— my mother wrinkling her brow from time to time as she reads, so that her whole scalp seems to shift as she concentrates

— my father hunting for his glasses which he pushed back on the top of his head

— people who look surprised when they laugh

5 JOHN HAS UNKINDLY POINTED OUT that since my spinal fusion my posture owes more to Groucho Marx than to Queen Mary. If he wants to talk to me while we are walking he has to overtake me to get my ear. It is one way of keeping ahead of him.

6 HAVING TO WALK THROUGH YOUR AUDIENCE to get backstage is a little akin to being a lobster swimming in a tank in a fish restaurant. The moment of being plunged into boiling water is not far away. Sooner or later these boorish swillers are going to devour you. Will they find you delicious?

7 A BOLD AND JOLLY OUTING to London's first satirical night-club by my former colleagues at De La Rue. Among them Mr Sawyer, who had shocked me at my interview by asking about my politics; but not Mr Far, my immediate boss, Mr Sawyer's second-in-command. It was Mr Far who had placed the advertisement that had unearthed me – in the *New Statesman* of all papers, while Mr Sawyer was away. Mr Far, who lives with a film critic and wears wonderful dashing suits, dark, but brown, not navy or grey, and with a stripe that is just a little too broad for even such a highly diversified company as De La Rue, and who will probably not last there himself much longer than I have done, was a kind man who went out of his way to be helpful in my newness; explaining by day all the words I did not understand in the foul language my friends and future colleagues-in-satire used by night. He made my job of glorified filing clerk as interesting as could be expected, but it's hard to see what the splendid opportunities were that it was supposed to open out for me in the fullness of time. Even allowing for the Day Release course in Economics that I was sent off to every Friday. I suppose I should be grateful to them. If it were not for the dullness of their job (as opposed to the entirely fascinating glimpses of the politics of office life) and my weekly Waterloo in the Albany Road Statistics class, as well as my own native impatience (or short-sightedness – the fear that I might wake up at forty saying: I might have done this or I might have been that . . .) I should never have plucked myself up to ask Peter and Co. to let me have a go.

Sawyer and Co. said that they enjoyed the show. He must at least have had the satisfaction of seeing me turn out, as he had predicted, a dangerous leftist subversive. No more adverts in the *New Statesman*, I'll be bound.

8 I GOT TO KNOW THE LITTLE OLD LADY dressed in black, who is always surrounded by a cloud of pigeons in Sloane Square. She invited me to call on her at any time – she lives five minutes from the Square – and when I did I found out why she is so tiny and so frail. I don't know whether she can afford to eat or not, but certainly she spends more money on the loaf of bread she offers every day to the birds than she does on herself. She was just sitting down to her own meal and apologised for having nothing to offer me beyond a cup of the weakest tea I have ever seen. She drank it to wash down her lunch of two Energen crispbreads, dry. I suspect she has the same for breakfast and for tea and supper. No wonder the birds are fat and she is thin. She must have some means, living where she does, but no interest in eating, beyond what duty dictates. She knows she ought to, so she forces those dry crumbs down her throat. There is a large dim living-room with a piano, covered with a chenille cloth, and a few photographs, but we sit in the kitchen and get some afternoon sun and the sight of a sooty tree in the back yard. Everything is musty and dusty. She has a strong Scots accent, bright milky-blue eyes, usually puckered in an impish smile, yellowing skin, with a few white whiskers on her chin. She cocks her head to one side as she talks. She is glad of a little company. I think she has outlived most of her family and substituted the birds.

9   *soothing things*

– a bedroom with a coved ceiling

– late at night, the atmosphere of a snooker club. Between shows at the Establishment we go to the Empire Club where, as well as the great green tables under suspended canopies of light, there are a few table-tennis tables at the back.

4

Concentration is high, voices low, murmuring against a background of the click of billiard balls and the faster but more muffled syncopated tap in the distance, of the hollow ping-pong balls. Faces are unimportant, except for the face of the man actually bent over his cue at the table. The heads of the others are lost in shadow above the pool of bright green. There is no liquor, but plenty of cups of tea and fried egg rolls, all night long

10   *delightful things*

– a young man running along the street to catch a bus; easy bounding gait, as if the pavement were made of rubber

– discriminating praise

– undiscriminating praise

– it is delightful when you can bring about a first meeting between two of your friends. Two keen and expert gardeners I introduced to one another held the conversation I had dreamed about (even knowing that I should never be able to follow it), walking through a garden, littering the gravel path with Latin names; still better was the almost inaudible discourse of my two softest spoken friends, who approached muteness in their desire to make least sound. If speaking too softly is, as Freudians claim, a strangled bid for power, these two are megalomaniacs

– globe artichokes; they are like an allegory, a metaphor for life, a proof of God; you work away slowly, leaf by leaf, tugging off with your teeth a tiny foretaste of the bliss that lies ahead; then when finally, after all your patience, you have won through to the last leaf – there is the choke; you have to make a supreme effort. The rich of course can go to restaurants where it's all done for them

5

11 ONE DAY ON MY WAY TO THE ESTABLISHMENT I reached the corner of Adelaide Road and Primrose Hill Road at the same time as a large white van and just as the lights changed against the van, allowing me to cross. It was fitted with a loudspeaker and as I stepped off the pavement a voice issued from it, jeering and calling out things like, 'Go back to the synagogue.' I was not prepared for their onslaught any more than I was for the violent rage which swept over me. In seconds I was at the side of the van, which I now saw belonged to Mosleyites, and had hold of it by the edge of the bodywork; and with might and main, wishing for the strength of Samson among the Philistines, I tried to over-turn the van. It was just as well the lights changed yet again and the van bore its delighted occupants away, still jeering, before I burst my heart.

12 A LOVER WHO PANICS does not inspire great confidence, though his temporary frailty and cries for help may endear him to you more than ever; and there is a certain allurement to be enjoyed in watching the normally collected, soph-isticated and discreetly superior young man go to pieces while you yourself, to his amazement (and your own), remain calm.

13 WE WERE STILL FAST ASLEEP in my attic room on the second-hand sofa bed I had bought for £20 at Peckham Rye, when there was a ring at the front door, five floors down. It was repeated and this time prolonged. I jumped out of bed, intrigued to know who could be calling at such an unearthly hour – it was about 10.30 in the morning – and fearing the worst. From my tiny balcony I could just make out far below,

the edge of a basket that looked familiar, and in it, the nodding heads of daffodils. Then a lean, tanned hand wearing a wedding ring was laid along the rim of the basket, fingers gently drumming. It was unmistakably my mother. I said 'It's my mother.' Whereupon the half-slumbering soul on the bed leapt as though electrified and began to gibber, clambering into his shirt. 'For God's sake!' he hissed, struggling. 'My tie! Find my tie!' I found his tie but could not keep from pointing out to him that although my mother might indeed think it a little off to meet him like this without his tie, she was observant enough to notice, and still more likely to take amiss, the fact he was as yet not wearing any trousers.

14 THERE SEEM TO BE A LOT OF LITTLE OLD LADIES in or around Sloane Square. On my way to see John in his sad bed-sitting-room I saw someone being very sick at the kerb, an elderly woman. It was a lonely sight. I went up to her and asked if I could help her, get her something to drink – tea, or even water to take away the foul taste. I was afraid she might be put out or offended but she was grateful just to have someone to hold on to for a moment. She didn't want anything but thanked me over and over again. As we parted finally she said, 'You're a real Christian.' I couldn't help feeling that that was rather a harsh judgement.

15 AN EXCHANGE HAS BEEN ARRANGED between us and a group in Chicago called The Second City. We leave at the end of September. Meanwhile one of the Establishment Club members, who is a travel agent, has arranged for us all to have a holiday in Yugoslavia!

16 ONE DAY IN ZAGREB, before taking the sleeper to Split and then the boat to Dubrovnik. We were shown all over the town with great pride and pleasure by a nice nervy woman called Dora. She has a strong sense of isolation, but it was hard to tell whether it was national or personal. We went into the great cathedral and from the back looking up the nave we could see an enormous hulk of a man, dressed all in black, kneeling a little to the left of the altar. John Bird said, 'It looks just like Orson Welles.' John Fortune remembered that they were indeed shooting Kafka's *The Castle* in Zagreb. 'It is Orson Welles,' he said, and added, 'but who can he be praying to?'

17 THE RIGMAROLE OF GETTING A VISA not merely to enter but actually to work in the United States, brings out all my contrariness. I curbed a silly desire to say that I was a communist; yet if I were a communist and determined to bring about the downfall of the U. S. Government and way of life, I should do likewise and say that I was not a communist. The medical was not quite what I had expected either. It included a blood test. I supposed that would be one of those little fairytale pinpricks, a drop of redred blood squeezed from your finger; but instead she strapped up my arm and stuck in a great needle and I felt very ill as I watched the huge syringe fill up with my good, rather blackish blood. Not wanting to let the side down I tried to hide my feebleness by making conversation. 'What's this test for?' I said brightly. 'V. D.,' she said crisply.

18 WHEN HE WAS A MERCHANT SEAMAN, Clifford told me, he was on shore leave in the Far East, and he and some friends fell foul of a group of youths, through a misunderstanding. Things were looking bad for them when a young man inter-

vened, with clear authority, and saved them. He insisted on inviting the Englishmen to his home where he lavished on them abundant, gentle hospitality. They were all enchanted with each other, and when the moment of parting came he accompanied them to their ship to take his leave of them. All were moved. The young man, with tears in his eyes, held out his hand to each in turn and said, 'In case we no meet again — Hello!'

I was reminded of this when I found a postcard this morning on the hall table, from Morocco, misaddressed, with the message 'Goodbye Rosemary! Do you remember me?'

19 WE LANDED IN NEW YORK IN DARKNESS as we had left London; subjected ourselves to Customs and Immigration insolences; but the officers' instant appropriation and bandying of our first names, and their cynicism at our projects, were muffled and filtered through our exhaustion and excitement. We waited for a bus to take us across the airport to the Intercity area — the Chicago plane. Our luggage piled beside us on a flat truck. The porter was indifferent, disabused; money would never wring a smile from him, nor cartwheels; he had seen everything and we were nothing; his life tasted of sawdust. We bestowed on him unfamiliar dollars; he disappeared and we waited. Limbo. The longest car in the world drove past us and we forgot our panic: that we were missing the Chicago plane.

We caught it. Heavenly contrast: the cool half-empty dimness of the Intercity line after the chartered flight — crammed, hot, running out of food, Nescafé, water. Here we could stretch and separate and sleep. A long leap and a landing; now one short bounce to the question mark itself.

20 AT O'HARE AIRPORT A GANG OF JUBILANT STRANGERS meets us, banners streaming in the night air and Union Jacks flying. It is a wild celebration. They introduce themselves, but we cannot disentangle them. They know who each of us is, they have studied our photographs and can tell us apart. There are only five of us, twelve or twenty of them. We bundle into several of the long long cars and speed off down multi-laned highways; words like DOWNTOWN flash past. At the theatre are more people – a party. Bourbon and coffee, with bands of whipped cream squeezed out of an aerosol canister, and hamburgers on black rye bread, served with a small sweet red apple and a heap of matchstick potato chips, downstairs in the bar: a cosy room, dark wood, with mirrors set all round at shoulder level, so that it is dark and light too.

21 THINGS SMELL IN CHICAGO that have no smell in London. The gas for cooking has a strange sweet intoxicating smell that nudges at you constantly, and having a drink of water is like diving into a swimming pool. We used to hear stories that some Americans were convinced that chlorination of water was part of a subversive political plot but it seems more likely to have been part of a Coca-Cola plot. On the other hand some things that have a smell in London have none here. We went across to the park for a quick visit to the little zoo there. In the Monkey House there was no smell of monkey, and no smell of lions in the Lion House, where we watched a three-legged snow-leopard limp restlessly to and fro like Rilke's tiger. She and the other great cats seemed to have been bled of their majesty by this hygienic purgation of their regal stench. Outside, where there is as yet no air-conditioning, I was grateful to catch a whiff of antelope and timber-wolf and good old fox.

22 WE ARE IN A GOLDFISH BOWL and our hosts are cats outside, occasionally scooping one of us out, in quite a friendly way, to examine us from all angles, before putting us back in the water so that we can go on behaving for their amusement. Most of them, though not much older than us, are on to their second marriage, or at least going through their first divorce. They don't ask, 'Are you married?' or, 'Are you engaged?'; they ask, 'Have you been married?' They are amazed that the three boys like girls. They thought practically all Englishmen were homosexuals, but especially actors.

23 THE WHOLE CITY SHOULD BE IN ANALYSIS. Almost all of our Chicago hosts are, and they are untiring in their efforts not only to treat us well and make us happy, but to find out what makes us tick, and how it can be that none of us is yet attending an analyst. They have named their little theatre boldly and affectionately The Second City, but the real city suffers under this epithet and cannot cease from trying to live it down and push it away — it is racked with neuroses, the principal being an undiscriminating, desperate thirst for approval. It cries out to be loved. We are constantly asked how we like the city. A disparaging remark, however slight or fond, becomes headlines next day. Meanwhile affection, curiosity and flowing hospitality threaten to overwhelm us, all five. It is not just a case of 'Eat! Eat!', but of be eaten too. New people are like food. They devour us. (More than the others I feel very much at home. People here may not be Jewish but they have absorbed Jewishness — they know about rye bread.)

24 THE SECOND CITY ACTORS WORK DIFFERENTLY FROM US. We sit round a table for the most part and decide on a topic, usually political, find a situation to contain it and then think up jokes to suit. They start with characters first, then situations and they get up immediately and improvise from there. What emerges can be funny, unplanned and organic in a way that our work rarely is (except perhaps the sketch I do with John Fortune about the boy and girl on a date) and their comment is social rather than directly political. Because of that they don't have such a hard time finding material for the girls. They suggested we do a workshop with them to try out their methods and we did have a go, but we were all far too self-conscious. We feel marooned without our jokes to hang on to; without them we don't trust the scenes to become funny. We have neglected our instincts perhaps — we try too hard. We did one scene in which I was playing a housewife and the doorbell rang. I went off to answer it, and stayed off. I was temperamentally and technically unable to motivate myself back on stage.

25   *irritating things*

— a faithful friend in the audience who tries to help the show along by laughing a little too soon and a little too loud. Our greatest fan in Chicago returns again, bringing scores of people. She has got to know the show so well that she now anticipates all the jokes, applauding innovations and revelling in mistakes. So she issues her wonderful remarkable loud low laugh — but always just too soon, obscuring the punch line and maddening both the audience and the struggling performers

26 WE ALL WENT SKATING in the local rink and the huge hollow space and the brightness of the ice took me straight back to the Wembley Stadium and my first fearful wobbly steps. Unfortunately time has not made me less fearful but more. My ankles felt ridiculously weak. Although I knew that, as in life, it is important not to be afraid to fall – that in fact you should deliberately fall a few times to get used to it (and wear gloves to protect your hands) – and although I knew that my spinal fusion will not undo itself, I was twice as frightened as I used to be; and being taller now and plumper, had further to fall and more flesh to bruise. Sad. But it's one of the things I should love to be able to do really well. Any kind of swift motorless movement, sliding, ballooning, sailing, skiing, freewheeling, has enormous appeal.

27 I DID A TERRIBLE THING ON SATURDAY NIGHT and shortened the show by about ten minutes. Three shows instead of two on Fridays and Saturdays is a lot. It can be exhilarating, but wearing too. Just before we went on to do the Couple sketch – of the boy seeing a girl home after their first date – John Fortune yawned and said he was getting a bit bored with the way he was doing it. 'I think I'll try doing it like Peter Ustinov, or no – better – Severn Dardern.' Severn Dardern resembles Ustinov a bit, bearded and substantial; he had been with the Second City and had 'gone on' like Mike Nichols and Elaine May, Barbara Harris, Alan Arkin. In the first and second shows I didn't detect any great revolution in his acting style as we looped our loops and convolutions of sexual embarrassment, trying to get to the point, any point; and the audience squirmed in appreciation. (It is especially nice doing this sketch here to a younger audience, because so many of them are actually on a date and may face a similar scene when they start home.)

When we came to the third show, however, it became clear to me that John was putting his plan into action. Instead of his usual light endearing diffidence, he was heavy, lethargic, slow on his cues. I got as far as asking him in for a coffee, but even that was hard to justify in the light of his new incarnation. Then, at the moment when, thinking of his long walk home, he said, 'Well – I suppose I'd better be going ...' there flashed through my self-righteous mind the knowledge that this girl would never have been interested in this man.

'Yes,' I said, 'I think you had better,' and put a premature full-stop to one of our best – and one of my only – sketches. The audience must have been mystified. It turned out that John Fortune was not being experimental at all – he was about to come down with flu and feeling very ill. I felt ashamed. It was almost worth it for the look of blank amazement on his face – but not quite.

28 Sidney who does the lights and the sound is a lovely man and very kind. When he heard that I was supposed to be writing a series of newspaper articles about Chicago for the *Daily Mail*, he at once undertook to be my guide and took me all over town: Old Town, New Town, the Loop, Evanston, a police precinct – though he left out the Playboy Club. He was eager for me to see and understand the city, warts and all and, of course, to love it. He is not tall or dark or remotely handsome, but short and fairish and a little plump. One day, a few hours before the show, John Bird was just about to enter the downstairs bar to cross to the dressing-room when he realised that it was not empty as he had thought. Sidney was there, all by himself on the other side of the room, looking into one of the mirrors, and John heard the words, 'Mirror, Mirror, on the wall, who is the fairest of them all?' There was a pause, and then an exclamation, 'Sidney who?!!! ...'

29 AN AGENT BOOKED US TO DO A SHOW at a school in Winnetka, Ill., for one of the school societies. We arrived in darkness at a place that seemed more like a city, or a university campus, than a school, and were shown into an enormous gym – there was a fine polished floor, ropes dangling down the walls but, although it was late, no seats as yet put out. 'Where is the audience going to sit?' we asked.

'Oh,' said our guide and went away to the side of the room. He pressed a button and one wall slid away and disappeared into the floor, revealing an auditorium for about 1,500 people. However, there were not above one hundred sitting there when the show started that evening, and many fewer by the time it ended. The booking agent had never seen the show but thought that as we were English our show was bound to be suitable for a family outing, which this occasion most pronouncedly was. At first the audience was impervious, and probably deeply bored both by Carole's songs and by our savage insights into British politics – and even American politics; but when we reached 'Strangler Martin' in his condemned cell, with Jeremy roundly dismissing the spiritual comforts offered by the priest in favour of those sexual ones that he could minister for himself – there really is no one to touch Jeremy for sheer relish in the matter of pouring forth filth – then the performance was punctuated by the staccato of clacking seats, as with each new oath or blasphemy, outraged parents dragged their unknowing children back up the aisle and out of harm's way.

30 A WRITER I ADMIRE teaches at Northwestern University. I plucked up my courage and telephoned him to ask if I could interview him for one of my articles. I was profuse in my apologies for disturbing him, if I was, and said that of course I didn't want to intrude on his privacy in any way. I knew

how busy he was both teaching and writing and that he probably had far too many calls on his time as it was. I bleated on in this vein at some length and he let me go on. I suspect he was enjoying something characteristically English about my approach. When at last, finally, I ran out of reasons why I should not be calling him at all there was silence. Then he said, 'Well. You must at least feel a little ambivalent about it.'

We talked a lot about which writers we liked – or rather I told him which writers I liked and asked if he did too. He laughed and said, 'You're a funny girl. You come here to interview me for the *Daily Mail* and ask me about Montaigne.'

He was surprised that the *Daily Mail* might be interested in an article about him, and he was right as it turned out, they were not. But they were not interested in any of my other articles either.

31 THE THREAT OF RAPE is the nearest thing to a welcome that Washington has to offer, plus one obscene telephone call. The three boys are in great demand already by the secretaries at the White House, and are invited to parties morning, night and noon; but Carole and I are strictly *girlies non gratae*. It is a city of transients, and of the unenfranchised and the discontent. An enormous number of the population are just passing through, by the very nature of their jobs. The people who live here permanently are shut out because they are not allowed to vote in the Presidential Elections and are not represented in the Electoral College; and we two girls are not allowed to walk even the three blocks to the Theater Club, for fear that we shall be knocked down, raped or robbed, or all three.

32 WELL — ONE FRIENDLY, WELCOME LETTER from a girl who went to my old school: just in case I don't know anyone here, or am not meeting people. Obviously she knows Washington.

33 THERE IS SOMETHING MONUMENTAL about doing a show to total silence which for months, and on two continents, you have performed nightly to audiences who gasp for air and clutch their ribs for the pain of laughing so much. Someone had the bright idea that since we were such a hit we should do an extra performance on New Year's Eve. The interval would fall nicely just around midnight and we could bring in the New Year in style, serving champagne and mingling festively with the audience. No one considered that the only people who would turn up on such a night would be the sad and the lonely, the left-out, the uninvited, the non-English-speaking. They sat (sixty of them) in consistent silence throughout the first half, while even those few really surefire boffo laughs which never fail, not with the duddest audience, sank like a Jeep through the ice-cap. The silence, the tension, became too much for us and in the end it was we who shamefully cracked, and we were the ones who could hardly breathe for laughing. It was a disgrace, but it was very funny.

34 WHEN JOAN ARRIVED IN NEW YORK with her two children her daughter Danny was spellbound by the automatic doors opening on their own accord to let them through. She gazed at them wide-eyed. 'It's magic!' she sighed.

An officer standing nearby replied, 'I guess you'll find that just about everything here is magic, little girl.'

17

35 HAVING YOUR FINGERPRINTS TAKEN MAKES YOU DIRTY and it makes you feel dirty – the way the mere fact of going through Customs can make you feel guilty. We all had to go downtown to be photographed and fingerprinted before we could become members of the Variety Artists' Guild, before we could be allowed to perform in New York City. You are not allowed to make the prints for yourself. A man takes hold of your hand; then he adjusts his grip to hold each of your fingers in turn, clamping them one by one by the first joint and rolling the ball of the finger in a pad of black ink, rocking it from left to right; then he takes the print, pressing it onto a special form with the same rocking motion. When he has taken all ten prints you are free to go and clean up, but you don't feel free.

36 AFTER THE ELECTRIC GLOOM of the License Office, what a relief to step into the sunny downtown street. The air was suddenly filled with white flying papers blowing across from the ticker-tape parade, celebrating Cooper's hurtle through space.

37 I MOVED OUT OF THE COSY ANGLOPHILE PICKWICK HOTEL and rented an apartment on the Lower East Side; so now that I had a kitchen it was high time to return some of the hospitality that had been lavished on me. I am not only nervous about my cooking but out of practice, and decided to keep it simple. I made my easiest meal, centred around my mother's recipe for halibut with sweet and sour sauce. It was delicious. The only thing missing was the guests: I was so nervous about the meal that I put off asking anyone until it was too late. I ate halibut with sweet and sour sauce for a whole week.

38 ON THE BOWERY one of the drunks was caught in the headlights of a car, which only just missed hitting him. He swayed on across the street, yelling, oblivious. Someone said they often get knocked down but, as often, escape almost unhurt because alcohol has induced a state of god-like relaxation.

39 I BOUGHT A BRIGHT PINK DRESS in a Mexican shop on Lexington. They had some jewelry and hair ornaments laid

 out by the till and I was amazed to see one of the little silver birds — are they baby eagles? — that my mother used to wear. Since I was small I can remember the very simple shape, head turned to one side, with a circle for the eye and a turquoise stone in the centre. I always thought they were Mexican–Indian. My mother had had three, worn as brooches, but somehow all three had been lost. The ones here were without pins, designed to be worn on a chain round the neck. I was thrilled by this find and by how delighted my mother would be.

40   *uncommon things*

— having a Russian russian teacher in New York who serves you Won Ton soup during the course of your lesson

41 WHATEVER AN 'OUTLET STORE' is, the ultra-fashionable Women's Haberdashers of Manhattan, before whose windows I drool, have one in Jackson Heights, close to where my aunt lives. She took me there and my eye fell at once on a great black cloak of woven wool, lined with red velvet, reversible. It weighs a ton and costs a fortune, a terrible extravagance at $100; but it is so rare to find any garment that I like entirely, without doubt or reservation, instead of the usual choice between mediocrities, or things that just miss, or have no flair; and the voice of the salesgirl always at my ear, 'These are very popular just now, madam' and 'they go with anything'. Going with anything usually means just the opposite, it's certainly not quite right, but at least it's not quite wrong.

42 IN THE CAB the driver, recognising my 'English brogue', asked was it true that the British Foreign Secretary was a pansy.

'It's all my fault!' I cried — that he should think so. Because we have only three men to play the whole of Parliament our sketch about the Cabinet, based one desperate afternoon on an outing to the pictures to see *Advise and Consent*, has me playing Alec Douglas-Home* in a man's three-piece suit, long hair and high heels notwithstanding. Now, compared with all that is going on at home, with John Profumo† *et al.*, it no longer seems absurd. Today there was a debate in Parliament — a vote of confidence for Macmillan.

Meanwhile as I struggle to learn their language, a man and a woman are circling above all this, speaking Russian fluently.

*The British Foreign Secretary at the time
†A Minister who resigned from the Government because of his involvement — initially denied — with a call-girl

43 WHILE I WAS WAITING AT THE LIGHTS a Negro — something wrong with his feet, something apart from bad, old shoes, like his worn, old cloths — came across the street, walking strangely in the rain because of his crooked feet, and carrying red geraniums in pots, using the bottom of a shallow cardboard box as a tray. Far too flimsy for all the pots. There was painful suspense watching him shuffle along, one of the pots pushing against the front of the box at each uneven step, so that it was about to fall out and smash at every moment. I was thinking just before I saw him of my wet feet and a warm flat and slippers. Finally he didn't have very far to go, just two shops along from the corner. And the pot didn't topple. But New York is full of these sad looming figures who appear, unexpected, unshaven, looking ill and weary or sly, to remind you that everything is not swimming, some things are drowning.

44 IF YOU LOOK OUT OF THE WINDOW there are always lights on somewhere in this city, however late it is. Very few people bother closing blinds or curtains unless they are directly overlooked, and you can see a block away somebody moving to and fro in an apartment. As remote as it is, it's very comforting, the spectacle of another human being up and about into the watches of the night. Another solace for the late-night lonely is the all-night radio programme. Why it should take courage I don't know, but I had to nerve myself to pick up the telephone and call the radio station and speak to the man; and five minutes later — at four-thirty in the morning — I existed. He played Gerry Mulligan's 'Festive Minor', 'for the English girl with the soft voice'.

45 AN EXTREMELY POWERFUL TELESCOPE has enlivened the evenings of a friend of mine whose apartment is high up, on Central Park. It is so powerful that he can see right across the park and into the domestic escapades of his fellow New Yorkers, and so clearly that he is afraid to breathe and give himself away. He has not yet found himself looking down somebody else's lens, but the other night he had the frisson of zooming in on a heaving mass of naked flesh and was riveted by the contortions of legs and arm, trying to work out who was which and what on earth they were doing. After a little while and a great deal of excitement he realised that what he was watching was one solitary man cutting his toe-nails.

46 TORONTO IS MARVELLOUS. I find it wonderfully peaceful after New York. But the boys are not so happy. Is a town where you have to sign for every single bottle of liquor that you buy (during those few hours that the special stores are licensed to sell them to you) ready for Satire?

47 THE AUDITORIUM WHERE WE DO THE SHOW is on the top floor of a department store and it is huge. In the evenings we pass between the shrouded costume jewelry and cosmetics counters and have to compete for the lifts with our smart audiences. (Smart — so far at least — in the English rather than the American sense.)

48 I DON'T LIKE HOTELS. The Ottawa motel, after the service flat in Toronto, feels very claustrophobic. It's not just the

extraordinarily sombre exercise in Japanese décor, the big windows all opening out onto the pool courtyard – I miss the sense of ordinariness I get from everyday purposes like buying coffee and yoghurt and strange new brands of cheese, and trying to find edible bread in this country – the supermarkets fascinate me. I hate not being able to make myself a cup of tea when I get in after the show; and much as I do enjoy being on my own, I liked chatting to Carole late at night over our tea, poring over magazines, listening to Dinah Washington 'Drinking Again'.

49 CANADIANS ARE EVEN MORE INSECURE THAN CHICAGOANS. I can understand a certain amount of Royalist pique at my opening address as the Queen granting Americans their Independence at last (although I think I play her very sympathetically), but who could have anticipated the outcry at the Phantom Pregnancy sketch, where the baby turns out to be a balloon? It has been interpreted in Toronto as a savage attack on Motherhood and on Pregnancy in general.

50 SOMEBODY TOLD ME THAT EIGHT OUT OF TEN PEOPLE who jump off the Golden Gate Bridge jump off facing the city rather than the open sea. I wonder how do they know this?

51 WE NEED HARDLY HAVE WORRIED OURSELVES about the 'hungry i'. All our nervousness about subjecting ourselves to the toughest of the tough, the most critical, the most sophisticated, to audiences that were used to the claws of Mort Sahl, was needless. It may have been the tourist season

of the year or simply that they, like us, had heard the name, and the 'hungry i' had become something to add to the San Fran list. Whatever the reason they could hardly be less interested. We wonder why they have come at all and clearly so do they — the disappointment is mutual. In fact we have not had such awful ill-mannered uninformed and disinclined patrons since we left Soho. Perhaps it was audiences like these that drove Mort Sahl to become a scourge of Society.

52 AM I THE ONLY ONE IN THE WORLD who is not enchanted by San Francisco — so European, so cosmopolitan? The San Franciscans are intoxicated by its beauty, its romance, its sophistication, its uniqueness; but to me the city is smug and self-absorbed. It is like Narcissus, leaning eternally over the bay to admire its own reflection. But right in the middle of its mirror is a prison.

53 I THINK I SHOULD DIE OF GUILT if I lived here long. Voices, echoes from childhood, exclaiming, 'What are you doing indoors on such a lovely day!' would drive me out to wander aimlessly in the balmy air, under these cloudless skies and I would go mad. It is Lotus Land. But in spite of fog, fruit, flowers, brilliance — all the physical aspects of the city, which continue to spring like a coil and to surprise you — all your first, happy homecoming impressions are soon contradicted. The hills are a relief after flat Washington and New York; but so much yieldless beauty makes you restless and melancholy. It's disconcerting to wake in this of all cities and feel no urgency about getting up, to prefer to lie in bed and write and read late.

24

54 I SAT UP FOR THE REST OF THE NIGHT after the show reading *Howards End*. It made me very happy. It is not a cure for homesickness, but it alleviates. Afterwards I hung out of the hotel window and watched the stars disappear and the sky grow pink. I determined to stay in bed all morning and damn the sunshine.

55 I FELT LIKE SPENDING MONEY — a rare feeling — but once I have made the first decision, broken the first note, seen the first purchases wrapped, something in me snaps. I kept away from the smaller shops on the whole — Gumps was dazzling enough for me. I fell in love with a necklace of grooved crystal beads, which are like drops of suspended light, and a crystal ball on an enamelled stand. I suspect I shan't bring myself to part with them. I bought a strange little metal man, from Peru supposedly and very old, also supposedly; and some coloured fruits and vegetables carved in ivory, with their creamy insides scooped out to show a Chinese scene: minute bridges, crossed by men carrying water-pails, while women below wash clothes at the edge of the stream. One, dark purple, in the shape of an aubergine, I bought for my mother in memory of our discovery of ratatouille. Several beautiful fans, a black one delicately painted — shall I be able to give that away? The question as always, what to buy for my father. Men are always a problem.

56 HOW WONDERFUL TO GET A LETTER. I read it in Union Square, which was full of men, on all the benches and a lot of the stone parapets surrounding the shrubs. Middle to aging men, in attempted suits, waiting, sitting. Where do they go when it rains? It is like a kind of bourgeois Bowery,

respectability strained after. Like the friend of my neighbour on the bench, in his brown jacket and brown trousers that looked as though they should match, but belonged to different suits.

— of David, plunging a knife into the centre of a half-slice of toast to clean it before using it for more butter, or honey

— of Judy, the smell of Listerine which she swills liberally before every performance

— of Jottie, cutting up garlic; she uses the very tips of her fingers and cuts it up incredibly fine

— of Flora, seeing someone lick a finger to turn the page of a magazine; she would be looking for a really good knitting pattern

— of Lillah, combing my eyebrows

— of Julie, cleaning the top of a tin before opening it

— of Pam, hearing a strange sound at the other end of the phone (which I finally identified as the noise of puffing on a Gitane and then exhaling); I wish she would give it up

— of my brother Gerry, the reflex action, when a driver brakes suddenly, of putting up a hand — safety belt or no — to stop the passenger being thrown forward

58 I FOUND A PRESENT FOR MY FATHER — AN INSPIRATION. I went into the store near Union Square, designed by Frank Lloyd Wright, to see what it was like. The half-circle entrance reminded me faintly of the Guggenheim spirals that make you feel as if you are standing inside some giant's ear. The

shop was frightfully exclusive, frighteningly expensive, filled with gold-plated inessentials – all beyond me I thought. Then I saw the perfect gift: a tiny bowl made of polished jade, a salt dish, and I remembered that earlier version of the King Lear Myth, where the youngest daughter is banished not because she says nothing, but because she says that she loves her father as much as salt loves meat. When, inevitably, he too is cast out by her sisters, she rescues him, by now become a blind beggar, and serves him a meal she has cooked without salt. In spite of his hunger, after the first mouthful he cannot eat: the savourless food reminds him of his daughter's words. As his tears fall on to the dish, his daughter reveals who she is and they all live together, happy ever after. I bought the dish and a tiny silver spoon, simple, curved, elegant, and felt I had done well.

59 SAN FRANCISCO'S CHINATOWN IS ALL YOU EVER HEAR ABOUT, so the Indian meal was a surprise. This was like stepping into another world. The room had a great gentleness. In spite of that magnificent tapestry tiger on the wall – what a reminder, he! – there was a great rest and peacefulness. And the politeness, graciousness, leisure; all these with a revelation of translucent flavours, far removed from any Indian meal I have ever eaten. Another world. And I am still drawn by restaurants and saffron-stained cloths, of student days in Cambridge and London. The mounds of yellow rice, the metal dishes of heavy curry, and lonely saucer of mango chutney, followed always by thick white cups of sour coffee and, if I was with John, a strawberry ice-cream. The rich and the less rich of India. My habit: English India, the British student's India. This evening, in the restaurant: wealthy India, the India of *The Music Room*, leisurely film I thought I hadn't liked, but it left its flavour with me powerfully.

60 THE GRAPHOLOGIST IN WELLFLEET, CAPE COD, former forensic expert, doing gypsy turns in vacation for pocket-money — a nice man. Brilliantly interpreted 'John' as I wrote him (meaning John Bird), as 'the leader of your group. You don't always agree with him, but you go along with what he says because you think he is cleverer than you are ...' I am curious to know what he would have found if I had written 'John' with another John in mind, or still another long ago John. John's a common enough name of course; and yet it does seem curious that so much of my affection should have gone always to men who are, somewhere, called John.

61 BACK IN NEW YORK I HAVE AGREED to be a woman 'Looking at Men', tomorrow morning on the radio. Up very early therefore for one of those vague generalising discussions that am not good at. It's all very well to say what you think but as soon as I do I think of an exception, or the opposite idea presents itself to me with great clarity and attractiveness. This time, quite on my own, with the others still out of town — it could be fun.

62 JAZZ MUSICIANS ARE EXTRAORDINARILY GENEROUS about each other. Perhaps because they never compete directly. They all seem to be each other's fans. Now that we are back at the Stroller's again the back bar goes on being a place of rendez-vous for writers, journalists, politicians, actors, directors, *le tout* New York, who stay on after the show, or who haven't seen the show (or seen it so often, bringing friends, that they have reached satirical saturation). But the musicians came in especially to hear Teddy, with Gene on bass and Fats* on

*Teddy Wilson, Gene Ramey and Eugene 'Fats' Heard

28

drums, when they move into the bar after playing out the second show; and now they come to hear Marian McPartland and her trio. A lot of them even I have heard of — Paul Desmond, Zoot Sims, Bobby Short, the Three Sounds. Gerry Mulligan heard me sing on the night that Carole was ill, and said that it made him feel very paternal (whatever that means); and Dizzy Gillespie bursts in between sets across the road: 'Eleanor,' he said, 'you bring me out in freckles and goose-flesh all over!' I bet he says that to all the girls.

63 OUTSIDE P.J. CLARKE'S, ON SECOND AVENUE waiting for Evelyn who is even less punctual than I am, I noticed a young boy, apparently waiting for someone also. When Evelyn finally arrived we went in and sat at a table in the back room and ordered lunch; and while we waited for that suddenly the boy rushed in and thrust a red rose into my hand and rushed out again. Without a word.

64 THE TAPESTRY AND THE TAPIRS distinguish the day — the Cloisters and the New York Zoo. Outside there was the Shakespearean garden, with heartsease and belladonna and rosemary. Inside, hung on the walls, the tapestry: fantastic invention. Besides the skill of weaving all those details into place: reflections in the fountain, not just of the bird bending over the pool but, in the wet stone of the fountainhead, the colours of the hunters' costumes; the way the water splashes into the pool; the ugly faces with evil eyes — one warted man; the foresters cutting down a tree for no seeming reason. There must be one, but what? And among all those flowers, the unicorn ... '*Où sont les pâquerettes?*' (Behind me two American matrons: 'When you think they had no central heating at all! I can't help wondering, didn't their hands get awfully cold ...')

The zoo too was crowded but we saw the tapirs with their curly snouts and short soft fur — strange elegance; and the rhinoceroses, amazing unblundering lumps; thick, grey, deliberate; tiny eyes and heavy heavy heads dragging down; great grey deformed unicorns. Apparently only a virgin can see a unicorn ... I suppose on the same principle that no one has ever actually *seen* an ostrich with its head in the sand.

65 I LOST MY NERVE ABOUT THE SALT DISH. That's a very obscure version of the Lear story — I suddenly thought my father might be bemused by this gift. I went into Tiffany's and bought some cuff-links.

66 ARTHUR THINKS I AM CRAZY to want to go back to London. The show has been a huge hit, we are a success. 'New York is wide open for you,' he said, 'a kid with your talent!' I was terribly flattered.

He took me to see a friend of his, an agent: he had the desk he had the cigar he had the smile. He looked me up and down and leaned back against all that leather and drawled, 'Well, Eleanor? What can you do?'

I gazed at him. I couldn't think of a thing.

'I don't know,' I said.

And of course from nothing, nothing — except a ticking off and a piece of sound advice from two old pros. 'You got to learn to *sell* yourself a little!' both men cried. And let me go back to England.

67 THE NIGHT BEFORE WE LEFT NEW YORK we all went up to Elaine's. Jim pushed his way along the counter to get served and I stayed put. The man next to me, hearing me speak, asked was I from England? He had been there once, liked it. And how did I like America? How long had I been here? How long was I planning to stay? 'I'm going back to London tomorrow,' I said. He put his glass down on the counter and gaped. He could not believe his ears. He spent the next fifteen minutes trying to persuade me that I was out of my mind to leave. 'A beautiful girl like you? You're crazy! New York is wide open! ...'

68 SO I FIND THAT I STILL LOVE LONDON. 'Still' is inaccurate. Before I left I was loathing the steamy crowded London, damp days of drizzle, and a thousand people pushing past each other in Oxford Street. But Thursday was wet like that and I didn't mind too much. And Friday — early, in Regent Street, with that pale sun and the bright scattered light in a mist, crisp air — was beautiful. There are twice as many people now, twice as many cars; movement in town is terrible. But what I loved anyway was the Heath, Primrose Hill, Camden Town, 31 bus London — spiral London, more than its centre.

69 THE CUFF-LINKS WERE A SUCCESS and the ivory aubergine, and my mother liked too the curious perspex trivet with orange and lemon fruits moulded inside it. As for the little silver bird — if it were not for the old snapshot of her reading to us when we were little, I should have wondered if I had dreamed them: when I produced the replica with a flourish, she reacted not at all. But that photo is so clear that you can even read the title of the book, *Who Goes There?*, and across

her dark dress are three birds clearly flying. So I shall keep it myself!

70 KENNEDY'S ACCUSED ASSASSIN was shot himself today by the owner of two Dallas stripclubs. Oswald murdered by Jack Ruby (*né* Rubenstein) and all that that entails, which is nothing. The police say, in their curious phrase, 'The Kennedy killing is closed.'

71 A BAD SHOW THIS EVENING. Little as I have to do in 'The Muffled Report', I do not manage to do it well. My timing is inaccurate, my characters blurred, partly because I do not enjoy any single one of them, have no affection for or belief in them, cannot present them succinctly. There is not enough variety either, for my taste. A pity. The boys too seemed dull, a slower pace. Plus a lot of corpsing – a bad sign. I must find out how to make a line funny to an indifferent audience not just a good one.

72 LAST NIGHT I WAS ASTROLOGISED and the astrologer gives me two and a half years of learning the hard way. The thorny future rose before me, bramble-covered, many scratches before the fruit. He talked about the left path – on which I continue, with my decision to go back to New York with the new Establishment show; and the right path – which I suppose I recognise, but invent reasons to neglect. By or on March 23 'things will become crystal clear ...' Two and a half years. I could welcome it if I had more faith that I would finally land up on the right-hand path. On March 23, to

crystal-gaze and take my decision, trust my neglected intuition. What if my neglected intuition tells me not to trust my neglected intuition?

73   *things that upset one unduly*

– the face of someone who has raced on to an underground platform just in time to see the doors close against him

– packing

74 SINCE I HAVE BEEN ON TELEVISION, LIVE, three nights a week, my brother Anthony says that going out anywhere with me is like going out with a motorbike – all you hear is 'Brn, brn, brn, brn, brn ...'

75   *things to which there is no reply (1)*

– the following letter, from Brighton:

Miss Bron –

Not a very good effort, dear girl – in fact a pretty lousy feeble one. You're not a bit like Sir Alec,* I'm afraid – too common by far. You are more like Nasser,† dear girl – same FOREIGN look.

You'll have to do better than this, girlie – what about Patrick Gordon Walker?‡ Now you DO look a bit like him, hook nose and all!

*Prime Minister at the time
†President of Egypt and the United Arab Republic
‡Shadow Foreign Secretary

Do leave poor old Sir Alec alone – he's very charming you know, and strangely, at least half we dull English happen to like him immensely. Why not have a go at fat little runt Wilson* – see if you can be un-biased, like a big girl should be. Try again – or get off!

(SIGNED)

– the following letter, from Hampshire:

Dear Miss Bron,

My husband and I feel we must just write a small note of thanks to you for the constant joy and delight you have provided each weekend on 'Not so Much a Programme'. Quite frankly we find much of the programme these days a bore but the moment you appear on the screen, in any of your many guises, I call out to my husband to come in from the kitchen or his little den. We are never disappointed! Your imitation of Lady Pamela Berry in particular is superb! We once met Lady Pamela and her husband socially and we have been telling all our friends ever since how good you are. Also if I may be permitted to add a personal word you are the only sign on the programme of good breeding and dignity with all those terrible grammar school boys and Jews. Keep up the good work!

(SIGNED)

77 THERE WAS A STRANGE FLURRY when I arrived at the party. Two women near the door flew into confusion and whispered to me, trying to contain their excitement, 'She's here!'

*Leader of the Opposition

'Who's here?' I was baffled. They seemed to be expecting some sort of scene or confrontation.

'Lady Pamela,' they hissed, with boggled eyes.

'Lady Pamela?' I was amazed. If they meant *my* Lady Pamela she was me, in as far as I had invented her character and I didn't know any other. Their Lady Pamela was evidently a real Lady Pamela and probably a real Lady, and unknown to me. Otherwise I should have taken care to choose a different name. But in fact wherever I go my own poor Lady is said to be 'just like' this or that Conservative Party lady, so whatever name I had chosen presumably there would have been some particular person assumed to be the model. The room was certainly full of people who talked exactly like her. I wonder if the real Lady Pamela would have been hurt to know that I had never heard of her? Mine would not — she is far too modest and self-effacing.

78 MY FIRST HOUSE-PARTY — somewhere in Oxfordshire. I did not know my hosts. I had been invited partly as a friend of friends and partly, I suspect, because they had seen me doing funny turns on the box, and thought that I should be 'good value' ... It all sounded very grand and rather daunting, though it began romantically enough, because I arrived at the small country station in a snow storm. It had started to snow in the early afternoon and by the time I could leave London snow was falling quite heavily and beginning to settle. As I stepped off the train the platform looked like a set for *Platonov*, with one light-bulb swaying and against it flurries of thick white flakes. I was wearing John's lovely fur hat and my black cloak and felt very Russian. I was met by a chauffeur in a Land Rover and driven through country lanes to the house. My train was late and, as there was no knowing how late it might be, they had not waited dinner for me. So

I clumped into the dining-room, still in my boots, upon a scene of great refinement and elegance: a long table lit entirely by candles, gleaming glass; guests in evening dress and friendly curious faces to inspect the new arrival. My host was charming and made me welcome, caught me up on my courses, fed me conversation as well as food and wine and did not allow me to flounder. But when the ladies were invited to withdraw I protested, daunted as I was. Everyone thought this was tremendously amusing (it was obviously just what they would have expected of me and terribly good value). But it was a feeble protest, unsupported. When the sexes were re-united in the drawing-room we played parlour games, mostly of the theatrical sort, adverbs and charades, and I was called upon in addition to 'do' members of the party. I demurred, which I suspect left the uncomfortable impression with them all that I could have done it very tellingly indeed, had I but chosen to. This was not true of course: a good ear does not make a mimic and a good ear is all I have.

I was grateful when bed-time came. When I went to my room I discovered that my case, taken from me in the hall, had been unpacked. My derelict underwear, a pair of shoes, a pair of trousers and a couple of sweaters had been put away in the cupboard; my toilet bag had been placed on the washbasin; and the unseen hands had laid the rest of the contents out on the bed: an elderly Viyella nightdress, an orange, and one glove.

79   *things which remain to be seen*

— a famous theatre critic tells you that if only you could bring yourself to bare your breasts in public you could play Cleopatra

36

– you go to an interview for a film; the director is charming and full of praise for your work on television but finally says, 'I think this part is too personal for you.'

'Personal'? You consider the implications of this for some months. Does it mean that your satirical associations mark you as superficial through and through?

81   *things that turn out differently from your expectation*

– you go to an interview for a film. The director and producer are charming and full of praise for your work on television; they are delighted that you are considering being in their film; they hope very much indeed that you will like the script; they will wait (eagerly, anxiously . . .) for your agent to ring *them*: they are offering you the part

– visiting friends in Wiltshire, an idyllic wooded valley. You are amazed to be able to hear the roaring of the motorway, which you thought you had left far behind. It is not the motorway at all – it is water rushing over the weir down below. At once the noise is transformed into a thing of romance, highly desirable

– turning up on the set of your first film to find that, yes, there *is* one of those canvas folding chairs out of Hollywood, with your name written on it – but: ELEANOR BROM

82 IT WAS WEIRD TO BE DRAWN INTO THAT MACHINE. I remember arriving back from New York and finding the papers full of photos of four boys with pudding basin haircuts and velvet collars. They were on the radio, on television, everywhere. Now at the press conference for the film I felt as if I were

several people, hearing my name bandied here and there, worse than U.S. Customs Officials. No I had not met them yet. Yes I liked their songs. Yes I was looking forward to meeting them. Yes it was very exciting to be working with them. Yes it was my first film. Yes I was excited – and very nervous!!! (Polite laughter.) Yes I was looking forward to going on the exciting locations, to the Bahamas and Austria and Salisbury. Yes I am a very boring person and will agree with everything you say ...

I did not say that before we got back from America I had never heard of them. Why do I always believe other people's interviews?

83 I DID AT LEAST REMEMBER that awful Establishment photo and leaned my legs to one side and crossed them very carefully so that they didn't squelch. How clever the Queen is.

84 ACTORS ARE ACCUSED OF BEING ARTIFICIAL but most journalists surely beat them for falseness – the bright smile-on-a-switch, the feigned interest, the lures and dangled baits, the sweeping searchlight of attention that hesitates, lingers, focusses: full beam, and moves on.

85 THERE WAS A SPECIALLY CHARTERED PLANE to take the whole unit out to Nassau and as we arrived discretely at Heathrow we were shown into a special lounge. Gradually our number swelled. There was an air of army exercise about it. The boys arrived separately, variously exultant or breathless as if they

had won through an assault course; and it was time to go. I was not prepared for the noise when we walked out onto the tarmac. It was Trafalgar Square with the volume up, beyond imagination – the sound of millions of starlings startled into the air. But the starlings were girls, when I looked back, very very young ones, who covered the airport buildings. Wherever you could see, wherever they could see, wherever they were allowed, and elsewhere, oozing and easing themselves in where they were not; waving banners and arms, pushing and heaving, in great danger I imagine of falling over the edges, wriggling and ceaselessly squealing – a high sighing hopeless poignant sound, unrequitable.

86 HUMIDITY MAKES ME CRITICAL AND IRRITABLE, quite apart from what it does to my hair – Nassau was a lot damper than I expected. We stepped off the plane into a bath of warm wet air, with lights flashing in our eyes and people calling out our names, first names, chiefly of course, the boys, to get them to look in that direction, this direction. 'Over here, John! Ringo!' From the airport to the hotel is like driving down a Raymond Chandler movie, oppression in the air, headlights picking out waving palm trees alongside the road. Everything seems lightly covered with slime; there is a feeling of wetness, decay, slippery things out of control; the air attacking the wooden buildings, peeling paint away from shutters. It's the kind of country where the wealthy would normally live up on the hills away from the damp and heat, but there are no hills here. Who would suffer such a climate for pleasure? Perhaps you could enjoy the sense of struggle against all that vegetation, beautiful trees, bushes, flamingo blossoms; but if you relax they will take over. Not as strong as the jungle, of course not, but that sort of imbalance. Nature doesn't want you here; and nor, I soon discovered, do most of the natives.

A breeze, though, makes things bearable, and the evenings are cooler. I am glad there is no clear sky and blazing sun, although it makes the tourist side still odder — people wandering about in gaudy clothes under a grey sky.

87 AMONGST ALL THE CLAMOUR of journalists and photographers it was an enormous relief to see my newspaper friend from San Francisco. Although he had written to congratulate me and said he would turn up, I had forgotten in all the turmoil. He hired a car and we drove to another part of the island not all that far from fashionable sinister Bay Street; run down, derelict, sad, strictly not for tourists. Very depressing; but wonderful to get away for an hour. I was surprised myself by the relief I felt at seeing someone, not even a friend, a warm acquaintance really, who had been however briefly a witness to another part of my life; a reality from which this present madness was far removed. His wry jokes and dismissiveness of his brother journalists made the madness absurd and funny and bearable; and of course he lives and breathes to prove that all journalists are not like that. The man from the *Daily Express* led the nagging and clamouring to get me into a bikini into the pool. (Bad enough in a whole bathing costume, let alone in bits of one.) They would not take no for an answer, in spite of the fact that that was the answer they got. I did a few interviews and was supposed to be able to tell them what it was 'like' working with The Lads — this before we had done one day of filming — and what they are 'like', after spending one plane trip with them. And really what it was like was like being a mosquito squashed on a mountain.

88 I MIGHT NEVER FIND OUT what 'they' are like but I found out what some other people are like – the swells of the island, upper-crusty; able to contain neither their curiosity nor their middle-aged spleen at seeing these four 'uneducated', 'lower-class' youngsters (products of the Welfare State) succeed. Who knows what manoeuvres they must have gone through for the privilege of being able to assemble at this scandal of a dinner given in honour of these mere boys, just so that they could turn their noses up at them; or – if they could thrust themselves close enough – to insult them personally, down their noses, with snide remarks; requesting autographs for 'demented' grand-daughters. And if they could not get close, watching from afar with pouchy eyes for proofs of callowness, social solecisms in unacceptable accents; so that they could relay these to the world, and their sense that they have been cheated – the shocking Ness of what the world is coming to.

What indeed, that it should have made them so far forget good manners and honesty and betray them into coarseness and the uncouth. Out of the mouths of elders and self-styled betters: pure filth.

89 A PHOTOGRAPH OF A GIRL IN A BIKINI appeared in the *Daily Mail*, back to camera, waving to Paul – squinting at her from a bicycle. The article alongside was headed:

BRON (quiet in dark glasses) THE BEATLE TAMER

My John wrote from London, 'A lot of people came up to me and said "Nice picture of Eleanor in a bikini" – even people who know you well. I had endless difficulty trying to persuade them that it was just a sub-editor's trick of subliminal persuasion, that you didn't wear bikinis, that your hair isn't like that, that if it was you they would have said it was you, and finally that, damn it all, I know what she looks like when she's got that little on and you'll just have to take it from me that it's not her. This last line, admittedly I have used sparingly, not on all and sundry.'

Out of all this I am struck by three things.

First: if journalists want a bikini shot they'll get a bikini shot, with or without you.

Second: the most surprising people read the *Daily Mail.*

Third: if I were built like the girl in the photograph there would have been no problem in the first place.

90 THE TWO DAYS' RESPITE IN LONDON were like blisters even with the relief of leaving Nassau and after long days of looking forward to going home. Home looked both wonderful and drab and sad. I could sink into it, but then there were the struggles to tidy it, clean it, refresh it.

91 IT IS EXTRAORDINARY TO SIT in a hotel room in Wiltshire making up and listening to that weird hysteria outside – hear it being confected. The girls are so close, standing just across the street from the hotel. They chant, 'We want ... ! We want John! We want Paul, George, Ringo.' And now a new call goes up, 'Look out the window! look out the window!' The crude whining imperative. Except there is no pleading – it's a demand for their rights. Rights of lovers? What? Just the constant human insisting unstillable cries and screams, massing, mounting shrill. (A glimpse of revolution – how if they were hostile?) But a lovely game they play, round and round, self-perpetuating, semi-serious, egging each other on.

A new idea now, anti – to enliven the old – 'Down with the Stones!' Insincerity in isolated voices, until they hear the effect of themselves on the others. Eerie, the fact of facing them like this, secretly across this dressing-table, with the curtains drawn.

92   *things that make you feel there should be one law*
         for you and another for everyone else

– the winding tree-lined drives that lead to great houses set in vast parklands and scarcely visible from the road; it is hard to believe that if you were to follow them the lonely landowner would not be delighted to see *you*; on the other hand, you might be a reason to turn the dogs loose

93 A LOVELY JOURNEY BACK to London in misty light, with our odd stop for Wellington's statue and that endless avenue. Sinister cypress trees added to a gentle pastureland, a lake, a landing-stage with rushes, trees and cattle ahead, where the long drive curved round – we never got as far as the house. And all in that soft drizzled light. It was totally apart. Like a chunk of time edged gently in to separate the days in Wiltshire from real things. These pages now have an odour of cat pee, since China's visit last night to my un-packed suitcase.

94 WITH THE LAST HALF-HOUR IN THE POST-SYNCH-ROOM today really was the last day. Not any regrets about that. A fine down thud. Petty farewells. Nothing to be compared with last Friday and Saturday, both lemon days, and myself being

crushed until oil from the rind ran with the sour juice. The slow pattern of our shuntings across that hollow studio stage, great barn place for a party, could have been a choreography. On top of all that vermouth, the drive to a jolly nightclub for a chosen few. Around all that part of the evening the drink was a halo. The rest was gradual tarnish, finally complete black, smudged over the shining possibility.

95 WHAT A TERRIBLE THING IT IS to have a hangover on a Sunday. At first you wonder whether it is a hangover or merely lack of sleep. Your limbs feel empty and discourteous. Everything is bleached. It is the end, there is nothing. Gradually, bringing horror, gray shapes of memories begin to form, of things blurted out in limousines; of a cabaret watched in a tormented trance, nudged by the edges of other people's boredom. Your self is spread out like the sheet you lie on. Thank heavens you remember some times like that in New York, that it is possible to recover from waking with the overpowering knowledge that there is no belonging, no attachment, possibly never, that might jerk you out of your white well. Thinking how terrible it would be to take to drink and wake every day with this thought, drinking to drown it, and become a lonely drinker with only drink to care about, or care for you. You slither about all day, deathly.

96   *vile things*

— Scrabble, which looks at language as if it were a branch of economics, turning the alphabet into a system of accounting and words into investments

— what happens to people who play Scrabble

– the death of fantasy: those periods when your imagination can't make any of your dreams end well, let alone happily

– wealthy landlords who put notices up on the railings in front of their properties that do not simply ask you to park your bike elsewhere: ANY BICYCLE FOUND CHAINED TO THIS RAILING WILL BE REMOVED AND DESTROYED WITHOUT FURTHER NOTICE. A week later, at least the words 'and destroyed' are neatly blacked out. They can afford good lawyers

97   *pleasing things*

– black olives, pale green peppers, spring onions on a plate

– a tiny tomato popped into the mouth and crushed

– unripe Conference pears from your parents' garden

98 It seems a good omen that *Howards End* will be the first straight play I do professionally. I remember what a boost it was reading it so far away in San Francisco; and my fright is mitigated a little by the feeling that I do know Margaret Schlegel and understand her.

99 WHEN ALL ELSE FAILS, I used to tell myself, at least there is always the certainty of knowing my right from my left. How ironic to go into the Theatre. Stage Right and Stage Left have me hopelessly confused. O.P.* is not much better.

100 MY FACE FRIGHTENED ME SO MUCH when I made up for the dress rehearsal that I nearly burst into tears. As it was I had managed to make myself look as if I were very very old and had been up all night crying. Passing L.A.M.D.A. external exams when I was fifteen has not stood me in very good stead – 5 and 9† are no longer the thing, apparently. Luckily Zena noticed that I was upset and in trouble and came and helped me, but I still can't get my eyes right.

101 I GAVE A LOT OF THOUGHT to how a cultured middle-class Englishwoman brought up, as Margaret Schlegel is, by at least one German-speaking parent, might pronounce the word 'garage' – which the Germans frenchify. So it is galling to be hoisted on this minute illusory petard by the critic of *The Times*, who chooses to pick on this tiny detail as if it were the clue to some devastating truth.

102 THANK HEAVENS THE SECOND MEETING with Forster was as different as could be. When he came to see *Howards End* the first time we were so much in awe of him that in spite of our

*O.P. stands for Opposite Prompt, the Prompter's corner being traditionally on Stage Left – I think it's left …
†Two grease colours, usually blended to make a 'normal' base

love and gratefulness to him, the atmosphere froze. We were all tongue-tied, or stilted and horribly formal – it was oddly like poor Margaret's lunch for Mrs Wilcox (a scene which isn't in the adaptation). But our goodbye lunch yesterday was very different, very merry, old friends. What a relief.

103   *disappointing things*

– finally realising how to play a part on the last night, after the curtain has come down

– having a ribcage like mine and not the voice to go with it

– a house without a piano

104   *things that are hard to resist*

– a voice on the telephone from Los Angeles saying, 'I'm lying here by the pool. Why don't you come out for a few weeks and lie here too, while I make my movie?'

105 LYING BY THE POOL IN THE L.A. SUN is not much of a life if you've been brought up in the Protestant work ethic, and happen to hate swimming. You can't even go for a walk here – there is nowhere to reach, and before you got that far you would be stopped as a suspicious character. I feel more than ever ugly, the ugliest girl in the world, drifting around on the edge of the water in my blue leisure gown. But the new Byrds record blasts out across the water and is beautiful; and the ice-cream machine is a great success: Banana + Peach + Sour-cream Ice-cream – unbeatable.

— a gala fund-raising evening, both Marlon Brando and Paul Newman to attend; but you have not brought a gala dress. (Truth to tell, you have no gala dress to bring.) Your lover dispatches you to Saks with his secretary to purchase a gown. Pride makes you refuse to charge it to his account. Indecision makes you buy two gowns. One is white damask satin, long, straight, demure, with a tailored jacket and three large diamanté buttons; one is black, long, sleeveless, simple, but scattered with little falls of rhinestones. Which will he prefer?

107 THE BLACK DRESS FOR THE GALA EVENING. No glimpse of Paul Newman. Marlon Brando sent a telegram of apology and a lot of money ...

108   *poignant things*

— you are at a party with a group of friends, including the lover you broke up with six months ago, after three and a half years together. He asks what you are doing next and you reply brightly, 'Getting married.' You explain at once that of course you mean the play by Shaw (you are going to do a tour — Norwich, Middlesborough, Hull) and everyone laughs; but not before a look crosses his face that is mixed of such bewilderment and hurt and concern, and perhaps even regret, that you are sorry for your moment of mischief, because now your mind is full of little questions — such as wondering whether his is, too

109 I AM ODDLY EXCITED BY THIS AWFUL EXPERIENCE of Norwich. We are sandwiched — at the Theatre Royal — between two

films: *It came from Outer Space* and *The Life and Times of Nell Gwyn*, which makes our offering seem even more pedestrian and unappetising. Such a play! No wonder this is one of the lesser-known Shaws. No one talks to anyone, not even to themselves, Chekhov-fashion, but only at each other, or the audience. Edith is a brick wall of a character and I bash my head against her. But I enjoy it. Every evening I do hope to find out what to do, though I am lax and have not done any voice-work or exercise or anything.

110 A FEW MOMENTS AGO I CAME BACK ON MY OWN with a clear sky and a few clouds drifting across the dark, and then stars, and then the snow began again. Little light powdery flakes. Now, in this strange poky room, with another dark ceiling that ought to make me think twice about painting my kitchen deep blue, I danced a twining dance to the radio, alone in black.

111 WHEN I WAS TWELVE, on holiday on the Isle of Wight, a young Scots boy played me a record of Ravel's 'Pavane pour une infante défunte'. Introducing someone to a piece of music is one of the nicest presents in the world. It is amazing how much music I still associate with friends I have lost touch with, or passing acquaintances, or even people that I have never met.

| At school: | Marlene — Rimsky-Korsakov's 'Schéhérazade' which we used to dance to, until Frances introduced us to sterner stuff: Dvořák's New World Symphony |
| At home: | My mother — Chopin; my brother Gerry — Beethoven's Pastoral, Brahms's Clarinet |

	Sonatas, anything with a clarinet part – though often we were robbed of half the tune as it passed to another instrument
Cambridge:	Joe – Verdi's Requiem, Beethoven's late Quartets
Hospital:	Antony Hopkins on the radio – Beethoven's Archduke Trio
New York:	Mike – Strauss's 'Rosenkavalier', the Byrds
Chicago:	Carole – Dinah Washington, Della Reese, June Christie
New York:	Jean – Blossom Dearie, Nina Simone Teddy Wilson – 'Satin Doll', 'I can't get started', 'I'll never be the same'
Women in Love:	David Watkin – Régine Crespin singing Ravel's 'Schéhérazade' and Berlioz's 'Les Nuits d'été'
Bristol:	Michael Rothwell – Poulenc, Scott Joplin
Perth & Fermoy:	John Fortune – Brahms's Sextets, the Kreutzer Sonata
London:	John Bird – The Beach Boys, Bartók, Boulez (and via Boulez 'Bluebeard's Castle' by Bartók) Stravinsky, Webern but not Stockhausen
Manchester:	Alfred – Janáček
	Lionel – Walton's 'Façade'
London:	Howard – Randy Newman, Joan Armatrading, Così fan tutte

112 IF GETTING MARRIED IS ANYTHING like *Getting Married* I shall definitely give it a miss. I have just offered what I hope is my worst to this town, with aching tooth and throbbing jaw (and now I cram good nuts and raisins into myself to try

to forget my sorrow). Here we go a-moaning, though Sylvia assures me that all tours are not as bad as this. She really is ill, with flu, and still manages to be magnificent in spite of a raging temperature. And here I am, hale and hearty, put out by a journey from Hull to Middlesborough and a wisdom tooth cracking surface.

113 MY JAW SWELLED RIGHT UP YESTERDAY and at least it was a relief to know that there was something wrong, not just a collapse of spirit. (Though that is fairly far on too ...) But the mist lifted for a spell today in the middle of the performance: I got my two jaws to meet and could speak. What a thrill it was! I went swinging up again to the elation of optimistic Norwich days, when things still seemed possible and the performance was plasticine, not yet pressed steel. I was very grateful because this week has been bad, myself sour and pitiful, and the contrast was very sharp. It was a mitigation to think that teeth and general physical lowering could make so much difference. Something to note for all time. And the sight of my face and my vanity – both formerly swollen, the latter now sorely punctured.

114 WHERE IS THE LINE BETWEEN SPOILT AND STRONG? My reluctance to accept the offer of an extra week in exotic Brighton (the Management's attempt to make up to us for the doldrum of the North) was seen as treachery by the rest of the cast, with one exception. Perhaps they all stood to gain, or thought so, Brighton being close enough to London for visits from The World – agents and managements and fame; whereas I stood only to lose, with my uncertain rendition. But if the way the performances have been going

and what they say about one another means anything, their sudden enthusiasm for the play is beyond me — lovely Sylvia excepted, who does care, in the good way.

Arthur, the only other dissenter, and I were made to feel very selfish until we sacrificed our wishes to be the greater good. One actress who would have had the perfect alibi, since she was to be married on the Wednesday after the tour should have finished, insisted that marriage was no reason to refuse such an offer, and that her fiancé, himself an actor, would understand and wouldn't mind at all putting things off for one week more. So contracts were drawn up and signed; except that after all her fiancé did mind, in fact he was furious and refused utterly to postpone getting married, even for a play of the same name. Another actress had to be hired and the entire company spent irritable days in Darlington rehearsing her to play the extra eight performances.

115 BRIGHTON STRUCK ME BADLY THIS TIME. All the bad buildings and new buildings hit the eye — the beauty that was, being swallowed. But it's amazing how quickly we adapt to a surrounding. This room is a monument to all drabness and weary dreary life. Six wallpapers, rotten lights, shrouded to submarine dimness by pink satin shades, a thousand patterns to the eye and no pleasure. Tiny framed photographs from a magazine, floral arrangements by Constance Spry. (Who took the trouble to frame and hang them?) Sylvia, when she beheld the satin draperies and bedcover and the matching lampshades, could not contain her mirth and rolled on the bed laughing, insisting we were lodged in a whorehouse. But my dressing-room at the Royal has been royally done up, because Marlene Dietrich is expected soon. And that's what it's all about.

116 EVIDENTLY MY CONDITION WAS NOT TAKEN SERIOUSLY, or was simply not reported (too astoundingly unprofessional, perhaps): I finally agreed to do the extra week in Brighton if I could have a television set in my dressing-room and if I could miss the final curtain call. On Saturday night they were at last showing *My Father Knew Lloyd George* and I was not going to miss it. I could catch almost all of it after my last exit.

I was amazed when the Theatre Manager came knocking at my door as I was packing up my things, wanting to know what had happened to Miss Bron? Why was she not at the curtain call? Had she been taken ill? Apparently no less than several of the audience had complained (they had to stay to the end so why should I be let off?) or expressed concern. I found it hard to believe that I or Edith had been missed. I felt quite flattered. But if they were fans of mine (to say nothing of Johns Bird and Fortune and Alan Bennett) they would have done better to stay at home and watch *My Father Knew Lloyd George*. That really was wonderful.

117 MY TREAT ON CHRISTMAS DAY was to walk across the hill, bearing a bottle, to see Bill and Magda and the boys and loll about all afternoon with them. But when I arrived Sally was there – she had dropped in. She gave a great whoop, seeing me, and cried, 'Oh, Eleanor, you're just like me – nowhere to go on Christmas Day. Nobody wants us!' As if Bill and Magda are Nowhere, just a convenience.

118 SALLY BELIEVES THAT I HAVE 'DROPPED' HER because I now move in such glamorous circles and she is not socially sig-

nificant. But in fact is is because she is too threatening. She
wants my life. If I buy a new dress I want Magda to see it
at once. I feel that she will get pleasure from it as much as I.
But Sally would say, 'Oh, Eleanor, you are *so* lucky!' – true –
but in a tone that makes me feel that I don't really deserve
the luck or to have such things, and that in some way my
having them is robbing her. She is the same about people.

119   *remarkable things*

– my mother's total lack of vanity

– my father's sense of fairness

120 NOW THAT EVEN I have been on *Desert Island Discs*, it's
not so much that I can go no further – it's that I shall have
nothing to do while I'm on my way. I've so often passed the
time beautifully on a long drive by trying to choose my eight
records. Now I've chosen them and they were not those at
all. The reality turns out to be very different. To begin
with you're not allowed long-playing records, so instead of
Chopin's Waltzes, which become even more marvellous in a
mass, I had to choose one only. That's absurd – impossible –
heartbreaking. And – once you have gone through your list
and selected your particular best moments, which all happens
before the interview – you don't actually hear the records
played. Presumably the extracts are fed into the talk when
that has been edited. That really threw me, because you
would be in a completely different frame after you had heard
that lovely Schubert accompaniment im 'Im Frühlinge', than
if you'd just been maddened by 'Hey round the corner – Ooh

55

Ooh!' (I decided on that, to act as the grit in my oyster – to remind me not only of my misspent youth but also of all the lovely other things I could have taken if only I hadn't taken that.) In fact I found I took the idea of isolation too much to heart to pick some of my favourites – the one I had imagined would be dead certs, like one of the late Beethoven Quartets. It would make me feel terribly bleak and lonely to hear that all by myself on an island. Homer was my book, entire and bilingual, so that I could go on constantly intending to start up my Greek again. It would make optimistic reading I think, with all those heroes sailing across the wine-dark sea and landing on islands. For my luxury I thought at first a silver ladle, because they are so beautiful – useful too of course and even, sneaky thought, a mirror of sorts. (Would I want to see?) But in the end I chose a mature sycamore tree: company, comfortable to climb about in; and it would conjure England and the seasons.

It's a very clever programme. People are far more revealing about themselves when they imagine they are at a tangent and talking about extensions.

121   *heartwarming things*

– you are interviewed on the radio and happen to mention that you do not believe in life after death; during the following week the B.B.C. forwards dozens of letters from anxious believers concerned about your state of spiritual starvation and clamouring to feed you: pamphlets, poems, personal experiences, incontrovertible proofs – a hundred signposts to Salvation

– you are so delighted by one of the cartoons in *Punch* that you stir yourself to write away and ask for a copy or a print of it. Weeks later there is a ring at your front door and, as

56

"Now I see it close up it's really more of a dirty grey colour!"

well as the milkman, there is a young, bearded and very diffident stranger in a suede jacket, who mutters something which you can't catch. He repeats it, on request, at the same time thrusting a package into your hands. You realise that what he was saying was 'I'm Albert'. It is the cartoonist himself who has taken the trouble to come personally to deliver the original – beautifully framed

– you have met your favourite film star at a party; he seems quite sad when you say that you are leaving and takes your telephone number; he also takes off one of your silver stiletto shoes and holds your foot and admires your hairy toes. But you panic and leave anyway. You are in bed asleep when the phone rings, at about half-past three; it is he, inviting you to come back and play the bongo drums with him

− a vow made when you were sixteen in Paris, never to break a date again (after the boy you had refused to go out with, pleading sickness, had met you in a café with the man whose invitation you had accepted half an hour later). And now, years later, when your favourite film star still remembers your name and telephone number after a week, and calls to invite you to a screening with a few friends, you have a date to meet at the theatre with Robert, from New York, whom you hardly know after all. And if you had known where to get in touch with Robert − what price honour then?

− who has heard of such cruelty before, that when your favourite film star telephones one last time to ask you out to dinner, you are ill in bed with flu

124 A MAN I WAS HAVING DINNER WITH asked me what quality I find most attractive in a man. I said I liked to be able to make a man laugh. He laughed and I asked him what attracted him to a woman. He said he was always very sensitive to a woman's voice, and he quoted Shakespeare, from *King Lear*: 'Her voice was ever soft, gentle and low . . .', a low voice was what he liked best.

For the rest of the evening, whatever I said, however serious the subject, he laughed a great deal; and I tried to keep my voice on an even keel

125 WHAT IS HAPPENING TO N.W.3? A letter today, simple but direct, the script and message suggesting youthfulness if not youth:

Dear Eleanor Bron,
   I love you.
      Brian Angell

P.S. Could you do a sketch where you show
your legs, as I am a leg man.

How touching to fall like that, in the dark and in suspense.
Does the beloved, on top of everything else, possess that
crucial perfection that sets your pulses racing? And if she
doesn't ...?

126 MINI-SKIRTS ARE A DISASTER FOR ME. My legs are fine, as
it happens but now everyone can see that, because of my
fusion, in order to look as if I am standing straight I have to
keep my knees permanently bent. I shall have to stick to
trousers, go for classic roles and keep my legs for best.

127 DINNER PARTIES CONTINUE TO ALARM ME, but I was
delighted when an old friend from college invited me to one,
as I have seen her so rarely since her marriage. She managed
it all smoothly and with great grace, which did not surprise;
but it was a rather formal affair, which did. The company was
chiefly academic or literary, and as far as my two neighbours
at the table went, desiccated and dull. Nevertheless I was
horrified when at the end of the meal she rose to guide the
ladies out of the room and I said so, very loudly, reminding
her of all her old egalitarian ideas and ideals, as I remembered
them — as we had shared them. For such a progressive,
forward-looking liberal couple it seemed very reactionary
style. The gentlemen half-heartedly urged me to stay if I

wished, but everyone was embarrassed or irritated. I joined my own sex upstairs. There bladders were emptied and make-up repaired and then we sat in the drawing-room and drank coffee.

Someone wondered what in fact it was the men talk about after dinner that is so fascinating and so unsuitable. Filth was suggested, and finance; but I remembered another evening at the house of the parents of friends of mine, years before, another progressive liberal family where once again the traditional post-prandial sexual schism was manufactured. On that occasion too I disapproved of the practice, as lightly and politely as I could in the circumstances, as we all rustled off. In that house the sitting-room was directly across from the dining-room and when we were all comfortably seated the same speculation arose about what the men found to discuss amongst themselves. I offered to solve the mystery, very simply, by crossing the stone-flagged passage and listening at the door, and I went out to see how the land lay. I was in luck, for we had left the dining-room door ajar in our exodus, so I had only to stand to one side of it and see what I could hear. To my dismay what I heard was one of the guests, a political commentator, saying to my friend, 'Yes, but what does she want to do? Will she stay on television doing this satirical stuff? Or does she have plans to be a straight actress? What is it that she wants out of it all ...?' and he went on, apparently fascinated by the permutations of an actress's career, while my friend struggled to reply on my behalf. To have to bring this account back to the sitting-room was embarrassing enough; but worse came later, when my friend, whom the commentator had been grilling, told me that from where he sat he could see my face, reflected in the glass of a picture that was hanging just inside the door. I could be clearly seen and observed at my eavesdropping.

This story called forth reminiscences and opinions from the other women and the talk ranged over many topics and was a pleasant change from the dry dinner conversation. When eventually the men joined us, our host said with mock deference, addressing himself to me, that he hoped that they had not stayed too long away from the ladies. I replied that on the contrary they had not stayed nearly long enough – which although rude was unfortunately true. It had occurred to me for the first time that evening, that the traditional after-dinner parting of the ways may well have been devised by women, not men, to spare their own kind hours of extended boredom over their meals.

128 A MAN I KNOW MAINTAINS THAT CONVERSATION between men is almost always an exchange of facts, information; whereas conversation between women tends to be an exchange of personal accounts, chunks of experience. He is fond of quoting the woman who joined a group at a cocktail party and became incensed when she was told they were just saying that the trouble with women is that they always take things personally. 'What utter rubbish!' she cried, 'I never do!'

129 HELLO FROM THE GLENALLAN GUEST HOUSE – another show, another Shaw. All alone with my bestowed electric kettle, about to drink a blessed cup of tea and casting my mind over this *Doctor's Dilemma* and how desperately I wanted to do it. This time I can't blame the play. *Doctor's Dilemma* is far more interesting and funny than *Getting Married* and Jennifer Dubedat decidedly more complex than Edith. I still feel that somewhere, somehow, I could, can, will do it, but it is as if I must cross an ocean. I practise for myself, all the strokes, all

understood and mastered, but when the moment comes and I lift my feet off and leave the shallows, there is panic (Forster's 'Panic and emptiness'?); and haste instead of pace. It takes courage to take time, the right kind of time – which is, simply, the amount of time it takes; yet if you don't you risk being unreal and boring, and that is a real waste of time. And though to take too much time can be selfish, not to take enough is not unselfishness, as Max so cannily points out. It's like shyness, a kind of meanness – an upside-down, false thing, a refusal to take responsibility. I need to force myself to be confident, forget my short waist and make myself believe that everyone wants to see me – or at least has a right to see the character I am playing. Then I might be free to blaze, and that is what I need to do. I don't want tweezered comforts, I just want to find out How; why I am so far from swimming. I have this foolish notion that suddenly everything will go click and be well and me marvellous … others take years but I must be instant. I suppose it is the old fear, of being always caught out whenever I am confident and think – even at the back of my mind – that I can do it. At some points I really felt that I was going to. Well I may still. I'm so tired, tired, tired – that corset crushing me. Acting is bloody and stupid: look at me me me me – am I alright? Am I wonderful? But times there must be something more than that. And those times take time, and ocean crossings. Meanwhile – the Shaw must go on!

130 MAX COACHES ME AND COAXES ME and makes me laugh. It is very generous of him to spend so much time on me. Of course he has spotted my inability to deal with the fourth wall, so that when I am facing out front I modestly cast down my eyes and no one can see my face; if there is anything worth noting in my expression it is entirely lost. I shall

have to overcome it. It's not just that it feels so false to stare out there, it does seem awfully rude.

– you are drowsing in bed in your digs putting off getting up, listening to your little radio pumping out the early morning news programme. Then your ear is tickled to attention by one of those interviews with a Personality who is passing through town. Even half-asleep you find it hard not to be irritated by the 'humble' attitude of the actress concerned, who talks a great deal about how terribly lucky she has been and how she sees this new role as a 'tremendous challenge' which she hopes will really 'stretch her'. Her voice sounds just like every other actress you have ever heard. It makes you want to reconsider the whole thing. You vow never to fall into this mode. As you turn over, however, the dread word 'satire' pierces the net of Morpheus and your ears open fully to hear her say that, yes, actually, it is a bit of a struggle trying to convince people that she can go 'straight', but that actually *Doctor's Dilemma* is not her first straight part – she has done *Howards End* and *Getting Married* for the Prospect Theatre Company ... Well, well, well ... you always wanted to be an actress and now you are really beginning to sound like one – at least offstage

131 NO BATH FOR FIVE MINUTES because the water has been turned off. Ten-thirty – a grey day. The only reason I wish it were sunny and not cool, is that I could wear my sunglasses then, not bother with make-up, to put it on and take it off almost at once. Five o'clock matinée. I have been lying in bed for a long time, aching; arms and legs so heavy and poor

crushed ribs. Will I stand it, I wonder, or will I get used to it? I have been bending to and fro between determination and a kind of disgust. The first night seemed nothing to me. I was just glad to get through it. Not a disaster thank God; and not the miraculous triumph over past problems and future obstacles. It is a problem to feel all the while that I look a freak, that I am huge and stupid, things of that sort. The corset may help to make me look better, but it reminds me all the time that I really need it. Anyway, after I brooded about that for a while I did swing a little to the thought: here are three weeks ahead now to use and use and perhaps free myself a little more – from my other, mental corset. Good shape all round.

133   *things that fill you with a sense of virtue*

– ironing, exercises, paying bills, writing letters, making appointments with the dentist, making appointments with the doctor, making appointments with anyone to get anything done, making yourself sit down and read, get up and walk, not eat

134   *things that fill you with reluctance*

– ironing, exercises, paying bills, writing letters, making appointments with the dentist, making appointments with the doctor, making appointments with anyone to get anything done, making yourself sit down and read, get up and walk, not eat ...

135 THE CORSET IS LESS AGONISING NOW. I feel happier and less like a whale; and so the thought of doing the play in

London, possibly all summer (at the Comedy), does not appal me so much. Nothing good or great, but a beginning. I've just realised I've left my watch at the theatre. Tomorrow I shall have no idea what the time is ...

136 A BARE WEEK IN ITALY is little enough before we go in to the Comedy and it's such a luxury to be able to have a holiday and know that you are coming back to some work. So I have rather grandly refused to interrupt this interlude to go to Paris to see a man about a film. One of us would have to drive me at least to within striking distance of Paris, and the car then has to be returned. And all probably pointlessly, because it's to play an American, and I can't imagine why they don't *find* an American. But the film would be shot on location around Paris, which would be nice; and with Audrey Hepburn and Albert Finney; and the director is after all a different Stanley, not the one whose film I hated in Los Angeles. And in turns out after all too that it will be possible for me to fly to Paris on a Sunday to meet him, once *Doctor's Dilemma* has opened. As it is we spent almost the whole of today hanging round the Lerici telephone office waiting for the continental operator.

137 THERE WAS ANOTHER LETTER at the Comedy today from my unknown (self-appointed) father-figure. I recognised the hand. This time I took care to wait until after the performance before I opened it (I had read the first just before a matinée.) 'I hope you won't mind if I speak to you like a father ...' and so on. The general gist: that, in spite of the satirical context, when first I hove into the public view thrice weekly, his heart had leaped – here at last was the face, here was the voice,

here the intelligence; the first English actress who possessed all the qualities to give us the great French tragedies; a Bérénice, a Phèdre (and later still presumably, in the ineluctable fullness of time, an Athalie). Ah! With what excitement he had hurried to the theatre to see my Jennifer Dubedat; and Oh! with what a sense of let-down had he hurried away ... A lot more work needed yet, alas! On stage my voice seemed to be not sure, not flexible enough, it lacked variety and cadence; I seemed as yet unable, or afraid, to attempt the emotional heights; my movements were not as graceful and fluid as movements ought to be, and finally — *le coup de l'âne* — I ought to lose a stone in weight at least. I wrote to my would-be progenitor that, no — he was not allowed to speak to me like a father. Only my father was allowed to do that; and my father would have known better. He would have known that one of the reasons I had wanted to do this part at all was exactly that it was, for me, difficult, and that I should have to work on the many things of which I have all too little experience, such as being on stage at all. He would know that, having had no benefit of Drama School, I was taking lessons in voice production — to learn to speak audibly, let alone mellifluously — and a thousand other things. In short he would know exactly where I was up to and how to level his criticism so that it would help me, instead of making it still more difficult and very painful for me to step on stage at all. Finally he would have chosen his moment to make his points, and not thrust them upon me in a letter which I was likely to read only a few moments before having to go on. In other words my father was not a well-meaning bumbling old nincompoop.

The second letter was charming and contrite. 'Never again!' he promised, venturing to hope that I might forgive him and not hate him, and that he might be allowed to feel that I had lost a father-figure and gained, if not a friend, a persisting and devoted admirer; and signed, 'Your very humble Bumbler.'

138 SOMEONE HAS MISTAKEN MY RELUCTANCE to move on stage for repose – that much lamented theatrical quality of a bygone era, hallmark of Eleonora Duse. A wonderful gentleman, old enough, almost, to be my father's father, came backstage in a rapture, wanting me to play Mrs Tanqueray for him, in Pinero's play. He was a manager and impresario of the old school, and if I had not been so ignorant I would have recognised his name. He had seen Mrs Pat play the part and said that it was uncanny, I looked so like her in my Edwardian dress. He remembered every detail, every gesture of her performance. If I would agree to play it he wanted to mount a production in the West End – he would teach me her every cadence . . . I wish I liked the play more so that he might have seen her once again before he died – a ghostly performance; but, today, a ghastly play.

139 A DIRECTOR FRIEND FROM NEW YORK was in London for a few days and refused not to come to see the play. I was horribly nervous. I was glad that he was seeing it, but wished I didn't have to be there too. It was not, he said, as bad as I thought. He gave me only one huge, simple note: 'Take yourself on stage more.' That was more illuminating and useful – and possible – than a thousand fatherly exhortations.

140 AND FOR THIS CONTROVERSIAL PERFORMANCE one critic has nominated me his 'Most Promising Newcomer to the West End'.

141 I WAS FINALLY PERSUADED to sit for my portrait but when I turned up at the studio I found that I was not allowed to read, or talk, or even listen to the radio, and was required to sit perfectly still. I got bored and after about forty minutes I could bear no more and said I must have a rest. 'A rest? You've only been there five minutes!' This turned out to be, unbelievably, true. I refused to go on sitting, as I was obviously temperamentally, or physically, unsuited. Undeterred, she went on painting the portrait in my absence probably relieved not to have the obstruction of the living alternative always before her, and using photographs which I supplied out of guilt. I was allowed to look at it when it was finished, or as nearly finished as it could ever be. It could not in a sense ever be entirely finished because, although the canvas must have measured at least five feet by four, she had not managed even to get the whole of my face on to it. My chin was missing and a large expanse of my forehead. I thought that perhaps it was as well that I had given up. Had I continued to sit, my enormous presence might have prevented her getting anything but my nose on to the space. (She has abandoned representational art now and moved to abstraction, and I have refused since that time any requests to sit, from whatever source.)

142   *lovely, kind, thoughtful things*

– a lover, after an odd affair that has come to an uneasy end, sends a telegram to await and welcome you in a strange country

143 THREE WEEKS ON LOCATION IN PARIS is a delightful prospect; a combination (until I get to know everyone), of the

unknown and the familiar. I shall visit old haunts, go and see the Bisseliches family, go and see my 'Man with the Glass of Wine' at the Louvre, practise my French. I wonder if most of the unit will be French. I need some sort of coat so I have bought a Burberry for fashion-skiving anonymous chic. Unfortunately on me it looks more anonymous than chic. Perhaps drab is the word.

144 CHOSEN FOR ITS OLD-WORLD INDIVIDUALITY, but especially for its famous restaurant, this hotel is certainly old; and I can see Notre Dame from my window. It is also very noisy indeed. Apart from the traffic outside and the various clankings in the courtyard at the back, there is a creaking of ancient floorboards above my head at strange hours. Each room has a different décor. The basic decorative device of mine is seething redness. Red carpet, red counterpane, red curtains, red lampshade, but all redeemed by golden tassels, reminders of former splendour. The furniture, in palest green, has that antique look of best cracked paint, in keeping with the tradition of the period, which is probably Empire; there is not one comfortable chair. Already it is beginning to feel like home. But the restaurant is closed and this is a tragedy. Not entirely because the cuisine I shall eat will be less *haute*, but because I shall have to go out every evening. Apart from the fact that I won't feel like it after a day's filming, nothing is more soul-destroying for a lone woman than going to eat in a Paris restaurant and being treated like dirt.

145 MY HUSBAND IS SHORTER THAN I EXPECTED, i.e. shorter than me. His eyes are particularly blue. He is suffering from arrival pains and threw a fit when he saw this hotel, failing to see

the charm in dinginess. He wanted a real hotel with lifts and room service. Arriving is awful. He has never been to Paris before (perhaps not to Europe) and plop! from Los Angeles to this totally foreign place. He and his wife have moved to the Georges V.

146 FILMING IN FRANCE — from this limited experience — has points over filming elsewhere. The first difference is the wine that flows as a matter of course on location when lunch appears. No nipping off to the nearest pub, or bistro; no discreet bottles for the stars; great flagons are placed on every table. And in the *après-midi* the work goes on. The second, in the studio, is that there is no lunch. Instead of starting on the set at nine, so that you have to be up at six, to be picked up at seven, to be in make-up by eight, to be on the set at nine, filming starts at noon and goes straight on until seven or eight. There are no breaks, but everyone, almost, snatches a break for a drink or a snack in the canteen, when there is a gap for them in the proceedings. You don't get home at night that much later than you do when you leave earlier and coincide with the rush hour; and you have time to have supper and even learn some lines, without the pressure of having to get to bed early to be up in time for your call. And you can learn the rest of your lines over breakfast.

147   *pathetic things*

— a person who has a habit of self-denigration, but is clearly put out when others take him at his own word

— a woman who has taken just too long to understand that she is physically attractive, perhaps even beautiful; her beautiful sisters have had a lifetime to fritter away their inheritance; she has lost a legacy just the day after hearing the Will read

— trying to go back to the past. It is like going back to one of those drip castles by the sea, where you have scooped out the wet sand and dripped it into a grand or delicate palace. For a time it looks dainty and pretty and fine, then it begins to lose its edge and blur. You can sometimes add fresh sand, new outlines for a little while, but they soon fade, and it is fundamentally the old shape, receding, threatened by the tide

— you are trying to avoid a certain person at a party but the inevitable happens and he comes up and greets you with a condescending leer, saying, 'Cheer up, it may never happen!' and, 'Why do you always look so depressed whenever I see you?' You bite back the reply, 'Because whenever you see me I see you'

148 IN SPITE OF OUR DIFFERENCES during the run, I decided to show my affection for Malcolm by making him a cheesecake, from Nita's wonderful recipe. And if I was making one I might as well make three and give one to Norman and James as well. I hadn't time to wait long for the cakes to cool before I took them out of their tins, but just enough to tidy away the eggshells and wash up the bowls and spatulas to make as much room as I could for this delicate operation. With a knife I loosened first of all the pick of the three, the least firmly set, and gently pushed the push-up base from below so that the base came free and the cake was clear. But I had not reckoned with the hot rim dangling round my forearm like a giant bracelet and worse, the cake itself was balanced most precariously on my fingers' ends at an angle which made it difficult to land it. I cast about for a way to set it

down straight and free myself, and in that moment the cake itself acted, choosing its own kind of liberty by sliding from my fingers into an enormous bowl of stock, where it sank slowly until it was totally submerged. A few bubbles rose.

149 BEFORE WE ACTUALLY WENT TO CERNE I read up about it in some travel books. Aubrey de Selincourt:

All about Cerne are the hills. Before I went to Cerne I was told to be sure to see the ancient and mysterious Giant. Giant Hill rises precipitously just behind the town on the northern side; so up Giant Hill I went. I confess in my ignorance I didn't know then exactly what the Giant was like or where he was — and I couldn't find him. I climbed to the top and walked for a mile or two along that splendid ridge, still looking. But there was no giant ... we saw a notice near the church; it said the Giant could best be seen from a certain spot outside the town on the Sherborne Road. We went to the spot — and there he was, cut in outline on the flank of the hill — sixty yards tall. I didn't think much of him. The fact that he had been there for two or three thousand years didn't seem to make him any better.

And Arthur Mee:

CERNE ABBAS. Everybody knows its giant, like a sentinel of centuries in this countryside of the ancient monks. He is carved on the hill above the Sherborne Road, and his height is half that of the dome of St Paul's. He equals thirty tall men standing one on the other; each of his fingers measures seven feet, and the club in his hand is forty yards long. The chalk lines are two feet wide and are seen for miles. We do not know how old he is, but it is thought that he is linked with the mounds in which men lie who lived here before the Romans. Some say he was worshipped by our ancestors and offered sacrifice; some say he is a Saxon God. All we know is that he is very old and very ugly, and we are glad that he is now the property of the National Trust which will look after him forever on his hillside throne.

How interesting that both these gentlemen should be so snooty about this impressive relic and that neither in all their statistics makes any mention at all of one feature for which he is justly famous, not only in the locality, but all over the world – his fine upstanding phallus, fully commensurate with his majestic scale.

150 THE WEATHER, WHICH HAS BEEN SO AMAZING all this year and this month, continued to join in and present spectacles of beauty not deserved, bonus sights. On Saturday we drove to the West. It was patchy, cloudy. We climbed up the Cerne Giant, me full of peasant fears and avoiding His impressive parts. We fell into one of our wrangles, that seem so much less shattering and oppressive in the country than confined within walls. Inspired no doubt by the Giant I had a sudden fresh vision of sex – how little it actually has to do with its purpose, children. That thought cheered me, exasperated the saintly John. Before clambering about on the chalky slope we saw the Abbey, beautiful, with flowers out already, the last day of February; rhododendrons early and tiny white crocuses; and there was that one building with its roof all grown with ferns and mosses.

Then the best of the day, from Lyme Regis on. The sky clearing and slowly deepening as we drove. It seemed very English, the best part, twilight; the lingering departure of a good day, hardly bearing to tear itself away, and trees silhouetted against deep pinks and cool transparent blues and suddenly Venus there. All a great gift.

151 THE WARMTH AT INDIA HOUSE AND THE FLOW of pressing but courteous hospitality is overwhelming. Your many hosts whom you do not know, know you, and greet you and claim you and seem as delighted as they are astonished that you of all the wonderful people in the wide world should have seen fit to accept their invitation. An entertainment was planned further to honour the actors of the Prospect Company, some of whom were about to tour India: a gifted young poet was to recite some of her poems. The guests crowded into the salon and stood about, for the most part ignoring the rows of gilded chairs that had been set out, as if these were for far more important persons. And after a few moments the girl moved forward, tall and slim, wearing a sari of dull red and gold. She placed her left hand on the edge of the grand piano, as if she were about to sing, swallowed several times, pulling her chin in and staring down at the carpet. Then at last she raised her eyes and started to speak; but not for long. She faltered, stopped, started again, and stopped again; her eyes began to stray aimlessly; and then she closed them and sank to the floor. People rushed forward to her assistance and she came very quickly to herself again and drank a glass of water and was led away from the piano laughing and talking, as the company rearranged itself into straggling groups and clusters. There was none of the hushed tone, covering-over, or brave-facing that would have clamped an English gathering, as if the side or at the very least a self had been let down. Everyone was merry and matter-of-fact about the incident. It was taken for a natural thing. 'She was too excited,' someone explained. In fact her fainting away was almost a tribute to her sensitivity and sense of occasion.

152 A WEEKEND IN PARIS, WHAT ENVY! And I did enjoy it, with my classic approach to departure and need for justification: I said I would go and I went. Already the memory is very self-contained. The sweep of those wide grand stairs whose grandeur was matched only by the extremity of dilapidation – great swathes of peeled plaster and falls of masonry; pipes that ended abruptly, forlorn wires sticking out of the walls leading up to the dim flat with its spacious rooms and low ceilings which made for such gentle light. It had been a *palais* of this Marais district, which in wet February was living up to the name of the marsh it was built on. My brown fake fur needs shortening for Paris; it trailed along the pavement soaking up a solution of Parisian filth as I wandered about during the day while Gavin my host sat writing, prisoned at his desk.

In the evenings he made me read T.S. Eliot aloud to him, but interrupted me constantly to object to my excessive speed or my interpretation; or we had long chats in cafés while it rained on outside in St Germain-the-self-conscious; in the afternoons we sat in sunshine in the Luxembourg Gardens, gravel underfoot, mothers with prams, and he and I there languidly sucking caramels and settling the marriage problems of our friends; still uncontracted in any direction ourselves, in spite of his proposal in New York: 'If in ten years' time we are both still free ...' (No fewer than three men in New York put that same proposition to me. I must be the kind of girl men like to fall back on.)

153 GAVIN'S INSIGHT INTO MY TRUE NATURE though it has shocked him seems not to have closed the doors of his heart against me. In fact now in his glance there is almost a hint of tender concern as for one afflicted, that was never there

75

before. And I doubt whether he will take me to that particular restaurant again − or perhaps to any other − and I shall try to forget the name of it. I doubt whether I shall drink a glass of Kir either for a very long time. Cassis and cold white wine as an apéritif is very delicious, but one is enough and he should never have ordered another, knowing my head for wine, or for anything else. The said head was already swimming a little when the *carottes râpées* arrived, and the serious wine of the evening to accompany it and the steak. And it all took so long, and so many bottles of wine − that was the real trouble − so that although we were almost the first people in the restaurant we were still there when everyone else had passed our table at the window for the second time on their way out. And I was so full of wine and meat and spinach *à la crème* and tiny crisp *pommes allumettes* that I was really quite sincere when I refused a dessert, or so I believed. The waiters detected another note, or perhaps it was the experience of years that taught them always to push just a little farther, a little longer; or perhaps they really could not bear to see their trolley of fine *pâtisseries* and mousses and bavarois and *crèmes au caramel* and profiteroles and *fruits confits* and *tartes aux abricots* so decisively spurned; but it was as if they received some sign from their satanic *maître* at which three or four, or five of them − a weaving *corps de ballet* − picked up one dessert after another from the trolley and passed it before my eyes and nose.

'No,' I said. 'No thank you. *Merci, Non,*' and '*Non*' again. Still they continued to mark a slow-motion Sir Roger de Coverley in front of me until − perhaps almost anyone would have − I cracked.'Alright then . . .' I said. The waiters pricked up their ears. 'I'll have a dessert . . .'

'Which one would Mademoiselle prefer?' Oh Lord − how could I tell. Don't make me choose. Too late to draw back. And then, 'Why doesn't Mademoiselle try a little taste of each, perhaps . . .?'

'Well ... alright – but just a little taste, mind – a tiny soup-çon, *une miette* ...' A crumb of fourteen different puddings is still a lot of pudding. I don't know at what precise moment I crossed over the invisible line that had hitherto finely separated me from my own kind; how much or how little was still left on my plate before, very soon, I left Gavin behind in the land of restraint and decency, where appetite – at least this original kind – was a controllable urge. Gavin's expression – lightly puzzled, concerned, hurt on my account, just a little shocked for himself, quickly became the equivalent of an alcoholic blur. I was – what word can I find for the passing effects of compulsive eating: ingesticated ...

We were both grateful to get out into the cool air and walk a little by the Seine, leaving my tempters and tormentors cheerfully piling chairs on the tables after a good night's work. Another victim claimed: another addict exposed.

154 LOVELY BRISTOL. Kindness of people here, cheese entirely separable from biscuits, without fuss, time to spare to help. Towns on hills, with universities, with harbours. So far a happy San Francisco. Boats, cranes, downs. And a lot of words to learn.

155 I WOKE UP AND REALISED what a wonderful bed I was lying in literally and metaphorically. Clifford and Daisy's hospitality is 'truly perfect', as Jean Brodie would say. In the midst of it the letter from New York was marvellous, a solid centre of advice and tributary strengths:

'It seems to me the whole trick of Brodie, is to play her as a heroine; not a heroine in quotes, but a true heroine;

77

intelligent, charming, powerful, not visibly quirky. It's by her acts that her students and audience should come to realise, late in the play, what she is. Not by her manner. It seems to me mistaken for an actress to tip it from the beginning. That leaves no possibility of mesmerising or catching the emotions of the girls because she becomes too much of a 'character'. It's not unlike that lady, whose name I forget, in *The Longest Journey*, the one who says, 'Your stories are bad, but ... but ... but ... ' Brodie affords the most interesting possibility, namely, that she can take us in completely and then betray us. Unless they insist, I would suggest that you use an absolute minimum of Scots accent. She is a woman first, last and always concerned with personal power, which cannot be achieved in life without charm, awareness and, most of all, connection with other people. Hope this is some small help, although God knows it would be more fun if we could talk about it. I am deep in the middle of making a movie, and although I have a headache, I love it a great deal. And you.'

 – passing your driver's test, liberating yet imprisoning. It frees you and lets you roam and is a grateful release – though that sort of release from a dependence can be oddly sorrowful, emancipation plus loneliness. But what could be more lonely than woman the adjunct? And driving affords great pleasure in amongst the trials: lonely roads – a herd of calves driven by a small blond boy; gliding down the Cheddar Gorge in drizzle, wonderful grey skies behind pale spring leaves, unlit; and all this alone; without necessity to converse or exclaim or acknowledge. The reward is silence

 – John Berger's comment in the essay 'Permanent Red', which applies as much to acting as to painting, that 'Imagination is

not, as is sometimes thought, the ability to invent; it is the
ability to disclose that which exists'

157   *things that fill you with hope*

– you are low and apprehensive about the evening's performance so that you must make a great resolve; and you
do – take a swing and strike – and it really clatters along! It
is not the best performance, and a few elements get knocked
over as you go, but still you feel fresh and you are finding
things; you realise that although there are bound to be many
times when you won't manage it, it is a relief to know that
everything does not depend on the level of your soul and
the number of bubbles there

158 'EVEN WHAT IS BEST IN US CAN LEAD TO DISASTER.' I had to
dash up to London for a fitting, and on a matinée day. I have
to have at least three wigs for *Bedazzled* including one blonde
and one red; but apparently my hair is too thick and too dark,
and my hairline too close to my brow at the temple. Their
suggestion for overcoming this difficulty was to cut off my
hair and shave the hairline. A fine solution for this job. What
of the next? or is this it?

159 THE FILM UNIT MOVES LIKE A LITTLE ARMY taking over
territory – often from willing and fascinated citizens, col-
laborating in the disturbance of their peace and trampling of
their privacy. I question the value of filming, but I love it.
Especially when the locations are exquisite and the weather
fine and you have nothing to do but sit in the sun and wait

for your next shot, which may not be today after all. Forget the days when it is freezing cold and wet and your costume is thin and there is nowhere indoors to sit and the next scene is very difficult … What peace.

160 I WAS IMPRESSED LAST NIGHT by my own clear ugliness on the great screen. It makes me feel almost merry — released at last from some obscure obligation. What? To struggle to be lovely?

161 OUTSIDE IS CHANGING, PERHAPS TO STORM; blowing chilly and the sky all over clouds, milky and insipid. Yesterday evening the walk was wonderful through Regent's Park; the flowers changed to hydrangeas, delphiniums, scabious, foxgloves, odorous tobacco plants; and suddenly one solitary symbolic tree of roses — a rose I've never seen with a deep pale pink bud that loses its colour as it opens and blows.

162 *things to be grateful for*

— not being a horse-chestnut tree in autumn

163 THE GREENGROCERS LOOKED STARTLED when I walked into the shop and saw the pile of new apples, and said, 'How wonderful! It always makes me happy when I see the first Cox of the year.'

164 WE TALK AS IF AUDIENCES have some moral obligation to come to the theatre, but it is up to us to make people want to come. It will get harder and harder to persuade them to make the journey, and harder and harder to keep the theatres open. If there is any obligation it is perhaps on the television companies, who reap the benefit of all those actors who have learned how to act in gusty reps all over the country. They ought in their own interests to contribute to keeping the theatre going. But if a well-known T.V. face brings people in, that is a start (and some of the best-known faces have seen plenty of seedy stage doors in their time).

165 PLAYING HEDDA IS LIKE MEETING A FAMOUS PERSON and finding her to be quite unlike her public image. Because Hedda's dissatisfaction lends her colour and power she dominates those around her and we think of her as someone very strong; but as I get to know her, her lack of strength astonishes me. I remember a conversation not long ago about the need to distinguish between a strong personality and a strong character. Hedda has a strong personality alright, but a very weak character. Her image is a powerful one because she turns everything to destruction and we always tend to mistake the ability to destroy, for strength. She has some good ingredients for strength: wit, intelligence, energy and instinct; but she is swept by impulse and fear; she has no control and small courage, moral or physical. Even her suicide is a debatable gesture. Mrs Elvsted – a pale personality – is far tougher than she is.

Still – no wonder every actress wants to have a go at her. She is the beast in all of us. Compounded of elemental urges, conflicting with almost everything around her, magnificent when cornered. And the play sweeps along, gears meshing inexorably, tooth by tooth. It's like a demonstration of the Greek idea of *Ananke* – Necessity: given these people in this place there seems to be no possibility of anything happening differently. That ought to be limiting but on the contrary it seems to make it infinite. I don't think I could get tired of it.

166 My favourite demolition firm was McWeeney Smallman until a friend came back from New York with a name he had seen and thought I should like even more: H. Gabler – Wreckers.

167 Gillian's dislike of me is obvious but it is hard to tell whether it is based on personal aversion or on principle. It must be very hard to have spent so long in the theatre, drama school and repertory, and then to see some relative novice brought in to play the lead you are now almost too old for, just because television viewers of Worthing or Bristol or Newcastle will recognise the name on the poster and be enticed into their local theatre. Perhaps Gillian is always sour. Meanwhile there is a chill wind of disapprobation that blows from her corner of the rehearsal room, when she is required to be there, which undermines me, and makes me feel that I must be right to be so uncertain.

168   *things that are not nice*

– 'nice' people, who are so afraid of upsetting others (and of not seeming nice) that they are unable to be straightforward; their protectiveness puts the wind up their victims, who until now had no inkling that they were in need of protection;

their own oversensitivity makes them so afraid of being hurt that they become preoccupied and paralysed by the fear of inflicting pain and for that reason wound, or at least bewilder, far more than people do who are casual, forthright and insensitive

169 ON THE SECOND NIGHT OF *Hedda Gabler* there were seven people in the audience, and the wonder is not that there were so few, but that there were so many, since the whole of the south coast was gripped by a blizzard. (Even if the car had started we should not have been able to drive home the few miles to Ferring. Roger and Merilyn and I went back to Eileen's digs and slept dotted about the house in odd nooks and crannies with whatever blankets and coverings her kind landlady could find.) But the performance was a wonder. Seven people concentrating so incredibly hard and we equally, so that our concentrations collided and fused somewhere over the edge of the stage and we became a unity. Why the Theatre is not replaceable.

170 WHEN MY RADIATOR THAWED the core plug fell out and left me stranded in Hyde Park on my way to Putney to rehearse with the Delmé Quartet. Working with musicians is such a delight; they seem to admire what actors do as much as actors (certainly me, anyway) admire their work. They maintain though that I have a romantic vision of them and perhaps my view of music is too ideal. To me a piece of music seems both more abstract and more concrete to work on than a piece of text – its wordlessness elevates it to some other sphere, makes it seem not earthbound. I suppose notions like these colour my picture of the musician as an initiate in some sort of religious order.

171 BLAIRGOWRIE SMELLS WONDERFULLY and powerfully of raspberries. A woman in the village told John Fortune's wife that she had left a few raspberries for her at the Lodge — twenty pounds ...

172 THE TWO OF US GIVE OFF GUILT like carbon dioxide, it's a wonder we don't suffocate, staring across the table at each other, trying to think of something to write, let alone anything funny, longing for eleven o'clock and the excuse to go downstairs and make some coffee and by then it will be almost lunch-time. We start off well enough each morning, scanning our list of themes and ideas that we drew up that first rosy tea-time by the library fire, when I had just arrived and everything seemed possible. But morning light is crueller. The room we work in is small and white and not intimidating, next to the nursery. We sit across a round white table about two feet in diameter, start off in the time-honoured way by sharpening pencils — he prefers a sharpener, I like to use a blade for a finer, firmer, more dependable point. We tidy the pile of paper we each have in front of us and consult the list each of us has made ...

At lunch in front of witnesses we are non-committal about our progress and hide our despair behind a pretence of urgency, an aspiration to punctuality, the need to get back to the desk. A little time to ourselves is allowed for necessary chores and then we meet once more, soporific and hopeless, completely demoralised by the reprieve we have just had. We look out of the window, which is at the front of the house, so that we can see who comes and goes up the long drive, hear the sound of gravel under the tread of tyres or footsteps. We identify the birds that sit out on the little gable, mostly wagtails, grey wagtails ... The conversation strays. We wander guiltily at first and then with recklessness into realms of gossip like wine: reminiscence, personal anecdote, philosophy. We decide to go for a walk, to get some air, and we walk talking furiously and laughing with relief at our escape. And it is always from these stolen guilt-stained hours that our best material emerges, when we have stopped trying. We are beginning to be hopeful that the series will actually be good!

173 UNEXPECTED INSIGHTS INTO IBSEN from this sottish Highland life. The short days and long black nights with nothing to do but drink and talk about your neighbours. Everybody knows everybody else's business, past and present and, within narrow speculation, future.

174 I SIT IN A FOUR-POSTER BED IN A HAUNTED ROOM, book on blue eiderdown, and around me light leafy walls of a room that overlooks the ravine and the river, seagulls flying even here. We went for a walk in the bright afternoon to the Polish Tree — one of the great beeches, where Polish pilots carved their names during the war. The land folds and flows here, almost all covered in that mossy greeny gentle yellow. Clear skies. Miraculous clarity — it really is as if you had had your eyes taken out and cleaned.

175 MARCH 13TH LEAVING PERTH STATION on the night train, tucked up in my first class I keep my annual date with my diary and I feel good. *La veille de ...* on the eve ... the next day. To be thirty — what relief! I should have thought anybody crazy who told me to expect the great and growing

excitement of the few months before; the last weeks — a crescendo of intoxication: how heady the thought of leaving behind me the miserable pains of twenty-seven, twenty-eight and that last devil, twenty-nine. A kind of freedom beckoning now; certain things will not be expected of me, some questions need no longer be heard, like marry or not marry. A mood of galuptious optimism falls upon me. I feel that from now on I shall be without apology.

— writing and performing a television series over six months which no one seems to notice — but people tell you how wonderful you were on, say, *Face the Music* or 'that panel game, what's it called? . . .'

— being present as a writer at a casting session for a T.V. play, and finding out that all your worst fears, about actors being cast by photograph, and definitely by type, are true

— now that theatres are trying to give better value for money theatre programmes are often stunning and engrossing, and also, quite often, more interesting than the play

— you are playing a very difficult role; as rehearsals go on the director is encouraging and after the first week he says that he is very pleased with the way things are going; after the second week he says that you have made great strides. When the play opens he seems really pleased and says that you have made a huge leap forward. During the run he comes again several times and each time praises the enormous advances you have made. Pleased and delighted as you are with each report on your progress, and knowing that of course you are very far from the summit still, you begin to shudder at the thought of where you must have been at the start

177 MARJORIE HAD WARNED ME that she and Harry had arranged a dinner party for my first evening with them, to meet some of their colleagues at the university. She described the guests to me on the drive back from the station. One of them, a Professor of Literature, was recovering from a nervous breakdown of six months ago. This was to be his first social engagement since his illness – hitherto he had refused to go out. I had mixed feelings when she told me that he had agreed to take this – for him, now – huge social step, only when he had learned that I was to be one of the guests; had in fact made this a condition of his acceptance. I was both flattered and puzzled by this and felt a bit awkward too – it seemed to put a lot of unlooked-for responsibility on me. We passed a pleasant afternoon gossiping and picking beans and marrows and raspberries in the garden; but as the evening approached I found that I was growing foolishly nervous. I felt that I had to live up to something, but I had no idea what; I had never yet met anyone who had had a nervous breakdown and was not at all sure how to behave, if at all; whether I was supposed to know, to acknowledge, ignore or encompass it.

There were four guests apart from Marjorie and Harry and me. The Professor and his wife telephoned to say that they would arrive late, and when they came there was time only for the briefest introductions and we went straight in to dinner. I was placed next to the Professor and my relief was great when the first thing he said, turning to me and looking at me very piercingly, was, 'I'm just recovering from a nervous breakdown, you know.' I was enormously grateful to him. This engagingly frank approach instantly swept all my worries away. Then he added, 'And it's all your fault.'

He enjoyed my state of confusion and dismay, in fact he seemed to relish it, saying again, 'Yes, all your fault.' At this moment his opinion was called for across the table and he turned away, but over the soup he offered me the explanation of my culpability. There were, he said, two things about himself that I should know. First, that he was a great fan of mine and had watched every programme I appeared in, and especially had enjoyed the programmes with John Fortune.

Second, he was, or rather he had been used to be, an incurable philanderer. Women found him irresistible; they always had; he couldn't help it; and he could not resist them. Especially he could not resist young female students. His position as Professor of Literature and Lecturer and Tutor left him open to constant temptation, to which he was in a regular habit of succumbing, and although he admitted that he was troubled from time to time by little twinges of guilt, these were feeble, and quickly passed. He was too engrossed in the delicious and constant satisfying of his many urges and desires, to stop and listen to any inner voices.

And then one evening he settled down to watch one of our programmes and was struck by a thunderbolt. 'Do you remember the one?' he asked. 'It showed a couple lying talking to one another and they quote a phrase of Rilke's. You remember?'

'Oh yes,' I said. 'The one where he says that lovers should be the guardians of each other's solitude?'

'Yes,' he said, 'that's it. Well,' he paused and looked for a moment haunted. 'Well,' he said again, 'I used to use that phrase. I used to quote it whenever I was ... you know ... It's a wonderful justification that, you know, for a married man trying to seduce a young girl. It offers you all sorts of sophisticated freedoms, very attractive to an aspiring young scholar of literature. D.H. Lawrence says something similar, but it was the Rilke that I preferred. I always used to quote it, you see, every time. And it always worked. And then I saw that sketch you did on the television ... Well! ... I cannot describe to you the horror. It was as though all the time, all those years, there had been someone else in the room, somebody watching, somebody listening, and laughing and noting down what I said. It's not, after all, a very common quotation, not something you hear every day. I can't describe the horror. I went to pieces. Completely ... and so you see it was all your fault.'

And before I could make my bewildered apology for this inadvertent destruction of a fine mind he grinned at me and said, 'I'm very grateful to you, actually. That's why I was so keen to see you. That's all. It brought me up with a bit of a bump; but I am getting on, you know, and it was all beginning to be a bit of a strain. And I do love my wife.' He smiled and sighed. '*Und dann und wann ein weisser Elefant,*'* he murmured. 'More Rilke.' And leaving the rest of his soup untouched, his gaze fixed on the flickering candle, he went on with the poem:

> *Und das geht hin und eilt sich, dass es endet,*
> *und kreist und dreht sich nur und hat kein Ziel.*
> *Ein Rot, ein Grün, ein Grau vorbeigesendet,*
> *ein kleines kaum begonnenes Profil —*
> *Und manchesmal ein Lächeln, hergewendet,*
> *ein seliges, das blendet und verschwendet*
> *an dieses atemlose blinde Spiel†*

178 THE PROFESSOR OF LITERATURE told me a story which might make a nice sketch. I think it was about John Cowper Powys — anyway a man who suffered from the most terrible

*and now and then a white elephant goes by

†And on it goes and hastens to be finished,
    just going round, that's all, just turning, nothing in mind,
A red, a green, a grey, drawn in procession
    a small profile that's hardly been begun.
And sometimes a smile is beamed this way,
A blinding smile, a smile of dazzling bliss being lavished
    upon this breathless, sightless, endless game ...

guilt; to such an extent that eventually he was immobilised by it and kept to his bed. His nearest and dearest were driven to distraction by this course and tried to reason with him, but he dismissed as ignorant their efforts to persuade him that he was after all no more of a sinner than any other man, and they despaired of finding any way to relieve his anguish. Then one of them noticed a small hole in the wainscot behind the bedhead, and hit upon the idea of hiding on the other side, in the next room. From here they shouted a pardon at him through the wall: 'John! Do you hear me? This is God speaking ... You know there's really no need for you to feel guilty, John ... I don't blame you!' Did it work or not, I wonder? The professor did not know whether the ruse had been successful.

179 HOW HARD BUT TRUE WHAT FLORA SAID: happier and more alert, the less you eat; sluggish and less alive and interested, the more. And still that stupid hand to mouth gesture to banish hurt, that hurts too. One solution – to veto parties, or veto yourself. I prepared a frenzied feast for my house-guest and his mathematician friend, nice large man who likes to eat. Cheese soufflé, soup, goulash, apricots, meringues and cream. Then I left to walk round the Outer Circle. Fifty minutes ...

180 I NOTICED FOR THE FIRST TIME that Brunel's bridge over the Avon at Clifton, which was not completed until after his death, bears an inscription: *Suspensa vix via fit*. The toll-man said that it means 'This bridge was put up with great difficulty'. Probably an understatement.

✣ God speaks through a hole in the wall

JOHN *and* ELEANOR *carrying a step-ladder. They stop at Simon's door, and try the handle. It is locked. They put down the ladder.* JOHN *climbs up.*

J: Simon? Can you hear me? This is God speaking.

E (*whispering*): Disguise your voice!

J (*whispering*): I am disguising my voice.

E (*whispering*): You'll have to do better than that!

J: Look – am I God or are you? Sorry about that, Simon. As I was saying, this is God speaking. Look – I want you to snap out of this, Simon. I want you to unlock your door like a good boy, and come downstairs and have your meals with the rest of us – I mean with your father and mother and Rufus and . . . Yes, but you see Simon, grown-up people can't really manage on seven grains of rice a day. . . . Well if your Daddy promises faithfully to try to eat only seven grains of rice, can he smoke a cigarette – just one? . . . No, he won't catch cancer – I'll keep an eye on him. I want you to bear in mind that your not eating isn't going to help the children starving in China – I wish I hadn't told you about them – I mean I wish your father had never mentioned it. . . . (*To* ELEANOR.) Can't catch what he's saying. . . .

E: He says your voice sounds just like his father's.

J: Doesn't that make your father a nicer man – that he sounds like God? And while we're on the subject Simon – don't you think you're a bit hard on him? And on your mother too? They can't help knowing that you think they're wicked – and it hurts them dreadfully. . . . Yes, I'm listening. . . . Want to kill who? . . . No, that doesn't make you a monster Simon, every little boy wants to kill his father. You wouldn't be normal if you didn't. . . . And to what? . . . Yes, well that's perfectly natural too,

181 AN ACTRESS I ADMIRE very much was in Bristol and came to see *Major Barbara*. She told a mutual friend that there are two kinds of actress: those who act from a soft centre and those who act from a hard centre. Watching me she had thought – there is a soft-centre actress who fears, perhaps because of her strong appearance, or her reputation for cleverness, that people will assume she is a hard-centre actress; so that to counteract this impression she is misled into demonstrating her softness, straining after it, which she need never do. She could afford the luxury of playing against it.

182 I RECEIVED A LETTER FROM THE POLICE, acknowledging mine:

> I thank you for your letter dated the 9th inst., enclosing details of property stolen from your motor car DOT 284D, and have to inform you that enquiries are being made regarding this matter, and should any useful information be forthcoming you will be advised.
>
> Yours faithfully,
GEORGE TWIST
(Chief Constable of Bristol)

183 THERE WAS A PIECE IN THE LOCAL PAPER about the theft which made me angry with the police because they have given out my lonely farmhouse address. This makes me feel wonderfully secure and protected! On top of that journalists began to telephone to ask for more — what had been stolen? It was after all only my change of clothes for a performance next evening at a concert in Bath on my night off; and apart from my journal, whose value to posterity is dubious and to the thief less than nil, and my much-loved flouncy woollen culotte dress, turquoise flowers on a cream background, the only thing of any worth was the necklace of ancient ceramic beads from Egypt, a present from Gavin. I added for good measure that I was very anxious because there was a thousand-year-old curse on the beads, which meant certain death to anyone who possessed them wrongfully. I hope that this may cause them to be hurled hot-handed out of some Montpelier window to land at the feet of a passing bobby; but more likely they are sunk now deep in Avon mud.

184 STANDING ON THE SUSPENSION BRIDGE, approaching sunset: water far far below with small, probably plastic things floating along here and there, bright blue and black; to one side a swirling, set up by some current near the sludgy ribs of the bank, circling scum. The cliffs of the Gorge seem pink; the bridge vibrates with each car passing. Notices announce help at hand for the despairing: call the 'Samaritans'. Think before you jump. He who hesitates – or telephones – is sometimes saved.

185 THE P.A.* TOLD HOW once, when they were doing some location shooting on the bridge, one of the assistants was trying to clear the shot of curious onlookers, who had gathered to watch the filming. One young man had been standing in the middle of the bridge already when they arrived and became fascinated watching the crew. The assistant asked him several times, very politely, to move along, but he was absorbed by the camera and the actors rehearsing and seemed not to hear. Finally the assistant abandoned courtesy and raised his voice, 'You there! Yes, you! You're in the way.' The young man seemed to wake up, and without pausing leapt up on the rail and jumped off the bridge.

186   *unsettling things*

– you wake up very early and decide to go for a walk on the Heath. When you reach the zebra crossing you notice some dark marks here and there on the white stripes; but it is only when you reach the pavement on the other side that you see clearly that they are footprints, of the left foot only, and understand that the darkness is dried blood. The prints con-

*Producer's assistant

tinue along the path for about ten yards. Then they turn off on to the grass and disappear. You keep to the path

187   *exotic things*

— a fox in the city; on my birthday I looked out of my window and saw a fox in the cemetery. A Japanese girl would have thought it was a fox fairy — a handsome ghost prince come to lure her away untimely to the next world; and in the heart of Toxteth, in Liverpool, Fritz and his wife leave food in their garden for the nightly visit from their personal fox

188 WHICH IS BETTER, an actor with immense control and flawless execution, whose decisions you dislike; or a technically inexpert, random actor, whose instincts seem true?

189   *sly things*

— an actor, knowing that the precious time is ebbing for video-taping the play he is in, and having only the long opening monologue to do, says 'Fuck!' when he fluffs or dries, or throws a little tantrum accusing one of the technicians of moving and destroying his concentration, so that all his shots have to be done again, eliminating his errors; then his colleagues have to achieve the bulk of the play in one take, warts and all

— a pretty young dancer who is not outstanding, rewrites the proverb that nothing succeeds like success. She decides, since she has not much talent and no technique at all, that she will get herself noticed for doing everything wrong. This does succeed: she does everything wrong, she drives everyone mad — and she is not sacked. How weird life is

190   *things which make you suspect that some things are not worth so much effort and/or suffering*

— Dutch gardens, force-fed with flowers, a blaze of incompatible colours, superlatively uneasy on the eye

— Venetian glass; you watch the craftsmen plunge to the furnaces and back again, blowing, pulling, twisting and dabbing molten glass with wonderful deftness and delicacy, to produce an absurd coarse little clown or a garish ballerina

— your nephew's incredibly realistic impersonation of a dentist's drill

— at the Queen Elizabeth Hall you spend almost an hour of the precious rehearsal time trying to balance the sound for *Façade*; at the Bracknell Festival the following summer you perform it in a tent without any preparation or attempt at acoustic testing. The result is identical: half the audience hears every word, the other half nothing

— you lose weight for a film and are as thin as you have ever been; but you discover that although there is less of you you are still the same shape all over; and on screen your chest looks very horribly bony

191   *loathsome things*

— teasing; if it is aimed at you you have to have a sense of humour to bear it; besides this there is an art to teasing which very few possess. Practised by an expert it should make you feel wonderfully loved and included, reinforced — even as it gently tugs your feet back to within reach of ground; but it is used too often by the inexpert as a defence or cover, and it is not for amateurs. It can be a very blunt instrument and practitioners should have earned the right to use it — it is always in danger of confirming its victims' worst fears about themselves and cutting them off entirely. Although you know this very well, and hate being teased, you can rarely resist doing it yourself, to others

192 AN INTERESTING OBSERVATION WAS FORCED UPON ME on the set the day after I had been subjected to a particularly ferocious teasing. The lighting cameraman had started up on the very first day on location, saying he could see he was going to be very disappointed: he'd thought that when I came on there'd be a lot of laughs. Another day he would tell me to get my great hands out of the way — they were so enormous that when he looked through the lens he couldn't see anything else. He's a nice man and all this I know was part of an attempt to put me at my ease. Anyone must have been able to see how nervous I was. But he evidently could not see that he was making me worse, and on the baddest of days he went too far, managed too neatly to hit on all my silent terrors, which brought me close to tears, in a giggling hysterical sort of way. I gave as good, I thought, as I got — getting a bit shrill there on the way; and — here is the observation — when I saw him next day my stomach did that odd old renowned flip which I had long associated with being in love, or with some fatal primitive vertiginous animal manifestation. Here it felt like fear. And the parallel fascinated me. Afraid in both cases? And of what? Of revealing the true state of things? Well, in this case, of actually crying in front of everyone, senselessly and stupidly — of looking a fool. But I suppose I was afraid too, in New York all those years ago,

precisely of giving myself away whenever I caught sight of a particular blond head at the other side of the bar in the Strollers. Someone on the set must have seen that I was upset and spoken to him, because after that day he never teased me once, but treated me like an old chum and talked about sailing. It's not easy to tease someone on a subject about which they can claim total ignorance.

193 ONE DAY WHEN WE WERE WALKING to the Colombina d'Ora in Soho, I took a postcard out of my handbag to show to a friend I was with. It was from a friend of ours who had gone to Guyana. As I handed it to him he said, 'You have beautiful wrists, you know.'

I laughed. 'Don't be ridiculous,' I said. 'They're enormous.'

'Yes,' he agreed, 'but your hands are so big that that hardly notices.'

194 A YOUNG MAN JUMPED OUT OF AN E-TYPE JAGUAR and hailed me warmly. 'Don't you remember me?' he said. 'I'm a friend of Dudley's.' I couldn't really tell whether I remembered him or not. He asked me how Dudley was. I told him I thought he was in California. He asked me how long I was here and said he would come to see the play and would I let him show me the sights of Blackpool and could he take me to dinner — why not tonight? At dinner he admitted that he didn't know Dudley at all, or hardly. He had played in the same band with him a few times at Oxford. What a nice young man. He is the second this year to leap out of a sports car and claim to know Dudley. (Ron took me to the Boat Race.) They don't seem to realise that I hardly knew Dudley either. I wonder if women are jumping off bicycles on Sunset Boulevard and accosting Dudley, claiming to know me?

— you have flown to Spain, where your director is on holiday, for a hasty and urgent consultation with him about some scripts for a new series. While he is reading what you have written you go for a stroll with his friend through the village, which is on a hill, picturesque and whitewashed. As you pass by a high white wall you hear a clamour of children's voices. You speak about your sense of oppression in this country, the starkness, the aridity, the constant presence of the Guardia, the sense of a love here, almost a longing, for Death. The streets are deserted. The only person you see is a woman dressed all in black, a shawl over her head. You would like to buy some oranges and try, in your few words of Spanish, to ask if there is a shop. She points to her mouth, which she opens to reveal toothless gums, as if to say that she cannot speak, but then bows her head and seems to indicate that you should follow her. You agree with the friend that it all seems like something out of a film, and while you are exchanging these few words the woman disappears as if she had never existed. The two of you continue walking in the empty stone streets where the houses almost meet overhead. At the corner you see two big wooden doors propped open, like garage doors, and it looks as though there are large baskets outside that might contain produce. You hurry forward. Inside, a huge pig is hanging by its hind legs, its head almost touching a bucket into which its blood is dripping. You decide it is a Buñuel film

— you go for a walk in the very early misty morning in Regent's Park; you are crossing the metal bridge next to the boat-house and on the other side of the bridge, perched on a low branch, you see a peacock, tail almost sweeping the water. You decide it is a film by Fellini

196 WE HAVE LOST A FLOWER through joining the Common Market. Now only five flowers make a bunch.

197 *things you could do without*

– fish-eye lenses used for publicity stills (or anything else)

– being told, when you are whistling away happily to yourself, that you sound like a performing pig in a circus

– you are in the middle of a dismal tour, a shoddy production, tatty sets, a good play being mashed and a sense that the audience is being cheated; you escape for the weekend from dreary digs, between Lytham St Annes and Birmingham, and arrive home in the small hours to find your lover full of sleep and put-downs. 'Oh, it's you!'

198 I RECOGNISED THE PORTER at the Midland Hotel and he recognised me, from years before, and we greeted each other warmly. It was comforting to see a familiar and friendly face. He told me with some pride that he had been promoted to Deputy Head Porter. He took me under his wing – quiet care all week. It was a relief each evening to get back to the hotel from the shabby production, and be looked after. On the day I was leaving I went to the desk to make my farewells. 'I've come to say goodbye,' I said.

He became very serious. 'I want to give you something,' he said, and he took a small silver disk from his pocket. 'You can wear it round your neck with all those other things. It's looked after me for twenty-five years, since I was in the Navy, and now it'll look after you.'

It was a St Christopher, an old man with a staff wading through waves, with a haloed child on his shoulder. I was astonished by his gesture and incredibly moved and uncertain now whether he would be offended if I were to tip him.

I said, 'I don't know what to say. Thank you. Thank you very much.'

He looked put out. 'Well – you've got to give *me* something.'

'I beg your pardon?'

'Something off there.' He pointed to the chains around my neck.

'What do you mean?' I said.

'Well – I've given you something, now you've got to give me something.'

'But I can't give you any of these,' I said. 'These were all given to me by people. You wouldn't like it if I were to give your St Christopher to someone.'

'Well. There must be something.' He looked even more put out and a little cross.

I looked down at my trinkets to see if there were anything at all that had no weight of association. There was only one that had not been a gift and clearly now I was bound to part with it. I said, 'Well – I suppose you can have this . . .' and very grudgingly removed from its chain and handed over to him my little Mexican-Indian bird, with its turquoise heart. He was delighted. And I hung the St Christopher in its place.

199 ANOTHER HEART to hang on yet another chain around my neck. (There are so many now, from that one string of twenty-first birthday pearls from my mother, and the free metal fish for Pisceans off a *Woman's Own* magazine that Magda was throwing out.) People seize upon the chains to talk about – admiringly, aggressively, curiously. It is a demonstration of style, very revealing. It must be like having the kind of name that invites comment, to see whether people

can resist or not, and if not how not. But this heart is the most beautiful and strange, and sad too, because it looks as though it has been shattered centuries ago. Dark-grey stone that I cannot recognise, but the grey is only solid in one corner; the rest of the heart is threaded with white veins that make little cells, like a citrus fruit cut straight through, and one thread through all these is a dark red. I told John that it was like our relationship and he gave his hollow laugh.

200 WHY WAS I SO DISTURBED by the quote from Boulez saying that there is no such thing as happiness – only energy to stop you from seeing? Suicides are simply people without the energy to prevent their own lucidity.

201 WHO IS ALLOWED TO DESTROY HIMSELF? George Sanders because he was bored; a man I knew who blew his brains out – the aristocratic way – because he could not afford a chauffeur any longer. He knew the value of life, and of the dramatic gesture. Hedda would have approved, and of his reasons.

202 WE WERE TALKING ABOUT SUICIDE and a psychiatrist friend asked Dorna if she would ever think of committing suicide. She said she was already committing suicide, and had been for a long time, very slowly, by not having children.

203 DORNA INSISTS THAT THERE IS ONLY ONE SIN and that is not loving someone enough to be perfect — that is to say, to obey them perfectly. Starting of course with your parent, or parents. Adam and Eve did love their single parent — as much as any uncomprehending child, in those first days of life, does love the Being that feeds and succours it; but if you disobey that Being it is akin to not loving it and this — seeming not to love duly — is the strongest spring of guilt. This is the real Original Sin.

God's case, and the case for all parents, is that Creation is itself the greatest proof of love. Parents put themselves out to feed their children, whom they have created. What they do not weigh in the equation, however, is that their own food *is* these same children. They have made them, they are privileged to watch them grow almost from seed; they water and weed them and at the same time, as they watch them grow, they devour them, they digest them. They cannot help it — they love them. But this experience of love is not without pain and so they require love in return (although if they are wise they will not expect it, since they themselves when young have failed so utterly in the same circumstances). The poor children meanwhile are left out of this altogether. They do the best they can, but by the time they have woken up to some glimmering consciousness and can begin faintly to perceive what is expected of them they are already hopelessly behind in the love stakes. Their parents are galloping ahead, heavy with love, spurred with boots and cruel bits by their unwitting offspring. By the time the children are old enough to understand what it was all about they are also old enough to be berating children of their own. And Understanding, and late-flowering Love for their own flagging parents, only weighs them down the more.

– a child crying insincerely

– going through cheque stubs with your accountant, which you expect will be a dry and dull experience, but is rather moving; as each sum is accounted for and you remember why and on what or whom you spent it, your whole life seems to flash before your eyes

– someone uses the phrase 'bedroom eyes' and you remember the first time you tried to put on false eyelashes, in New York, to go to a party after the show – you thought it would make you look sexy. You got them on alright, upper and lower, but all evening your eyelids kept sticking together, fast

205 WE WERE TALKING ABOUT SEXINESS and one man said, 'Nothing is sexier than a left-handed woman who co-ordinates well.' Is this true? I feel at a disadvantage.

206 IF A MAN TAKES OFF HIS GLASSES when he is talking to a woman it is a sure sign that he finds her attractive, or at the very least wants to seem attractive to her. He may make some pretence of cleaning them or not, or rub his nose or his eyes, or he may simply take them off because they suddenly become irksome to him, and it is generally quite an unconscious gesture. A man who does not wear glasses presents a wide variety of indications but no one clue so infallible as this.

103

– people who feel obliged to correct printer's errors in books (and then miss some ...); actual objections written in the margin, remonstrances and plaudits are intriguing

– people who sniff after speaking, usually when they feel that they have made a particularly significant contribution

– pedestrians at zebra crossings politely miming 'after you!' when you have just stopped for them

208 TWO JEWELLED LEOPARDS, very tiny, exquisite, at the Chinese Exhibition at Burlington House (and two jewelled and furred ladies behind me exclaiming over them, marvelling; and then adding, 'They could almost be lizards!')

209 ANOTHER GEM IN *The Archers* TODAY, a query from Phil. 'Did those lambs get off to the abattoir alright this morning?'

210 THE MINISTER FOR THE ARTS MADE an illuminating speech at the *Evening Standard* Awards Ceremony. 'Why,' he asked, 'do we go to the Theatre? What is it about live theatre that makes it so much better, more rewarding, richer, so much more real than any other entertainment? What is it? Well, I'll tell you what it is. It's simply this: that when you go to the live theatre you can *see* the actor, you can *smell* him, doing his own thing right there in front of you.'

– you are about to open in a play out of town. One of the cast finds a lovely hotel a short drive from the town centre, set in its own grounds, views of trees and sounds of singing birds, very tranquil and good for the nerves. On the morning of the opening you feel full of an unaccustomed calm and optimism. You find your colleague already at breakfast. He looks pale, but he always looks pale. 'I've just had an insight into the Nature of Love,' you tell him, affectionately.

'Have you?' He raises his eyes to look at you, and looks away again. 'I've just had an insight into the nature of diarrhoea ...'

212 WILLIAM WAS TALKING TO HIS CAT holding her up to the mirror above the mantelpiece and what he was saying sounded like a poem:

Why are you looking that way,
Staring into the mirror?
Why are you staring into the mirror and crying?
Is it because you think that I am not here any more?

Certainly in French it would pass as a poem:

Pouquoi ce regard
Dans le miroir?
Pourquoi te regardes-tu
Dans la glace, en larmes?
Crois-tu que je ne sois plus là?

213 LAURA HAD BEEN INVITED TO LUNCH BY HER LOVER'S MISTRESS whom she had never met. She thought the invitation absurd

in so many ways, but decided to enjoy the absurdity and accepted in a mood of devilment and mischief. She had no idea what her rival hoped for from the meeting, whether she would try to reason with her, attack her, or whether she merely wished to size her up, but she was ready for the fray.

I asked what the confrontation had been like and she laughed. There had been none, she said. Her hostess had, she guessed, had second thoughts because she had invited another guest, a woman friend, to defuse the situation, which, in effect, lacked all electricity. 'It was like stepping into a pool of water of exactly body temperature — one of those experiments in sensory deprivation. Of course sensory deprivation can drive you mad,' she added.

I wonder if she would have felt so sanguine if she had known that her hostess had tried to break down with an axe the door of a room where her lover was lying with (and to) yet another mistress.

214 *more things which you think you can do without*

— at three in the morning a telephone call soaked in brandy

— at three-thirty in the morning a lover soaked in brandy

215 *things which can do an actress no harm*

— to be befriended by one of the follow-spot operators; at the curtain call you feel the bright pool creep from its central station to spill a little extra glory over you, too; and Joan, back on a visit from Canada, who has never seen you on stage before, insists that you really do have that elusive star quality.

'I don't know what it is, Eleanor, but whenever you come on stage everything just seems to get brighter, somehow ...'

106

— in a bookshop, moving your recent work to a more promi-
nent position

— a well-dressed man, very early one morning, pinching
cuttings from the fuchsias in Regent's Park

217 THE DUCKS NEVER GOT THE BREAD, it was too mouldy — I
threw it away. The F.M. on my transistor is still working,
which you mended: I listened to a promenade concert and a
programme about the Beatles. I keep passing places where
we could have gone dancing. I remembered the name of the
book. The cigarette papers you looked for all morning, and
a little tobacco, were under some rags in my saddle-bag. You
never did anything about the creak in the swing. I went back
to the zoo. I play the record a lot. I have short sudden bursts
of tears. I must be very tired.

218 DORNA THOUGHT THAT I WAS LOOKING TIRED and asked
whether I was planning to take a holiday when the play
closed. It was the usual problem, I said. I needed a holiday
because I was tired, but I was too tired to summon up any
energy or enthusiasm to do anything about it. And I don't
really like going away on my own. And I don't really like
going away with anyone else. She said I ought to try what
she did, on the principle that a change is as good as a rest:
she had taken three days' holiday without budging from her
flat. She had made two rules — as long as these rules were
adhered to absolutely, anything was permitted. The first was
that she was not allowed to kill herself; the second was that
she was not allowed to feel any guilt, not cosmic and not

trivial. Whatever she did. She could eat drink smoke lust sleep read all day long lie in bed leave her hair unwashed not telephone her parents be a success be a failure do or leave undone any of the thousand things that daily gnawed at her — she was totally, temporarily, exonerated. After three days of this, living without guilt, she felt refreshed and actually exhilarated. 'But I don't think I could have kept it up for much longer than that,' she said. One thing that pleased her greatly was that it was also the cheapest holiday she had ever had.

— auditions; they thicken the air with fear and can damage the psyche. There must be a way to enjoy them — perhaps by managing not to care, not too much (being in work already) — but it is very hard to reach that liberating height. I have been lucky to have had to go through so few, although the alternative — 'meeting the producer/director' — also has its many horrors. But auditions can alter the personality and induce schizophrenia. Once when I had just left a show in difficult circumstances — my song had been cut — my agent, laughing, suggested that I 'go along and meet' the man who was doing the London production of a Broadway musical. I should have had the sense to guess that since the 'meeting' was to be at a theatre, it was not going to be a meeting at all. As soon as I went in at the stage door the atmosphere of suspended breathing and cold sweat told me that this was in fact an open audition. People were hanging around in the corridor with staring eyes and frozen smiles, and lining the walls up and down the stairs, talking low.

Suddenly my name shrieked through the air, and down the stairs rushed a rawboned redheaded body which threw itself at me and hugged me. If anything could have proved the splintering effect of auditions this effusion was it. The actress who had greeted me with such burning affection and such relief was someone who had been a member of the permanent company at Bristol some weeks earlier when the show which I had just left was opening there, before coming to the West End. She had made no attempt then to hide her disapproval of the fact that our company had been 'brought in' for the purposes of a West End 'try-out', which she considered unethical and an insult to herself and the resident team. Her withering remarks were relayed throughout the theatre, but I had no occasion to suffer them personally since she adopted a policy of treating the intruders as invisibles. (The women, that is; she ignored us totally, but did deign to speak to some of the male members of the cast, some of whom were very attractive.) It was clear that the audition had turned her brain, or at the least tilted her memory. I don't recall whether she got the part. Partly, but not wholly because, expecting a quiet interview such as had landed me my last role in the musical in which I now no longer was, I had come without a song.

I was not forced to hang around backstage with the rest, but was shown on at my appointed time, into total blackness, relieved suddenly by a blinding spotlight.

'Hi there ... em ... Eleanor! And what are you going to sing for us?' came from out of the blackness – the voice of the exhausted producer, who was going without any lunch.

'I'm afraid there's been some mistake,' I replied; and although the kind piano player begged me to sing – 'Anything! Sing a chorus of "Raindrops keep falling on my head" '! he pleaded – I scuttled off. Only partly to blame because if I had sung I think, in all honesty, I'd have stood even less chance of getting the role. Well – I should have been better prepared. But I was annoyed, with someone, for not making things clear.

— men with beards; try to discover why they have a beard —
shyness, a sense of chin failure, a striving for macho-dom,
weariness of shaving; if they are married, take care: a man
with a beard is often living a double life or uneasy in his
marriage, or just uneasy

— people who start their sentences with the words 'with
respect', in order to sound less abrasive and to conceal,
even from themselves, their own arrogance. Far from being
respectful or deferential it signals contempt for an unworthy
opponent and intellectual inferior. Politicians use it frequently,
and deliberately, for this very reason

— if you are a man, a woman who suddenly has all her hair
cut off; a strong sign of dissatisfaction, very likely with
herself, but it may be with you

221 AN INVITATION TO *Tristan and Isolde* gave me my first
opportunity to test my uninformed hostility towards Wagner.
I thought I should die of boredom before at last the interval.
But even I could tell that I could not legitimately make either
approach or retreat in Wagner Appreciation from seeing this
insufficient production. I could not decipher exact words, but
received a few strong impressions of what ought to have
been. Here I was presented with the spectacle of a man and
a woman who quite obviously could not bear one another,
lying uncomfortably on a mound and singing about love,
and physical passion in particular. And *Tristan* is supposed
to be the easy way into Wagnerland.

– it is New Year's Eve and you feel strong and full of
resolution that next year will be a good one. You look back
at the year gone by, during which in spite of a stretch of
seven empty months you were in one of the best Chekhov
productions in a long time – and now are rehearsing another –
you finished writing a book and recorded a classical record
which included some of your own verses. But as you think
about it all it begins to seem quite black and bad; all your
doubts about whether you did ever get there in that first role
begin to return, and whether you let the director down after
his huge leap of trust casting you. You find that you have
lost all belief in your book (who could find it of interest?),
the record, which you enjoyed making so much and thought
so marvellous, seems lost too, you feel a tinge of embarrassment thinking of it. And Christmas finally has breathed its
poison over friendly feeling, almost to the point of universal
suffocation. Of this quite good year nothing seems to remain.
All dust. Is this so? Or do you feel like this simply because
your lover has gone away without a word?

223 A NEW YEAR'S EVE SPENT CYCLING across London in
pouring rain when your lover has deserted you on some
flimsy excuse, or no excuse at all, ought to be depressing;
but in such a circumstance, when your hair is plastered across
your face and hanging down your neck, making a tributary
stream, and you are soaked beyond the skin and your wrists
are numb, you may look towards the New Year with a
justifiable hope that things may improve. If you are making
your way towards a bright warm room to eat fried eggs and
chips with old friends to whom you are able to offer a bottle
of champagne, so much the better. (Of course even under
these conditions, a puncture might alter your outlook.)

224 WHEN I TELEPHONED THE ANSWERING SERVICE there was finally a message, after ten days' silence; just to say that he had called. When she had passed it on the girl said, 'Are you going to marry him, Miss Bron?'

I said, 'Is it the wish of the Answering Service that I marry him?' and she said, 'Yes.'

I pointed out that he has never asked me and that he was the party and not me to whom they should make their wishes known. He is obviously wonderfully charming and considerate to them, and they assume that he is to me too. I should have recited to them my verse, dedicated to him, called 'No Answer':

I waited
For the phone to ring
And when at last
It didn't
I knew it was you.

Perhaps it is time to invest in an answering machine.

225 AT THE ZOO ONE EVENING I WATCHED the young lady rhinoceros having a fit of rage, or so it looked. Throwing herself about, charging up and down the compound, hurling herself into a tiny insufficient puddle and trying to make it bigger – kicking out a shower of stones, splashing the giggling humans, coating herself – not voluptuously but desperately – with mud.

At one point a mud tear trickled down her face.

— a lover who, having been himself unable to sleep, and finding that you have woken up, does not have the grace to let you sink, as you long to, easily back into your slumbers, but engages you in a discussion — rather one-sided — about contextualism,* until the outlines of the houses opposite begin to loom in the first light

— the expression 'good value' applied to a human being

— sending an anonymous bouquet of flowers to your lover's mistress

— emptying a carpet-sweeper (as opposed to a vacuum cleaner)

— picking blackberries in a graveyard on a wild day in summer, clouds scudding across a blue sky, while you are waiting to be called for the next scene

— a pair of scissors that works really well

— clothes that are so worn that there is finally no choice any more but to throw them out

— if there are two or more of you at supper, and artichokes, not heaping the leaves up neatly as you finish them, but hurling them all round the room (preferably backwards over your shoulder)

---

*Apparently contextualism is something to do with the context in which buildings are designed, used or viewed ... I am none the wiser

— a man leaves his wife in middle age for a younger prettier woman, and she takes it very hard. After a few years she shows signs of being quite mad. He is relieved that he got out when he did and does not have to cope with her; but, although he is not a nice man, he finds himself wondering whether she would have gone mad if he had not left her

— an old friend, who loves you, tells you that you must 'learn to like yourself more'; another old friend, who also loves you, tells you that you must 'learn to like yourself less'. Probably they are both right

229 SOMETIMES IT IS HARD TO SAY what I want in case I may be wrong in half an hour; no wonder I am wary of sustaining a part in a play, unable to sustain myself in the world. Convincing inconsistency is one of the most lifelike and elusive qualities an actor can capture. It is achieved more often by novelists — Forster does it for instance.

230 IN *The Encyclopedia of Murder* THERE IS AN ACCOUNT that Pirandello would have appreciated, about a lie-detector operator. He told of an interesting case, where a lunatic who claimed he was Napoleon was given a test. When asked if he was Napoleon he denied it, but the detector showed he was lying.

231 WE WERE TALKING ABOUT how well it is possible to know oneself. Margaret said that she knows herself very well, that

there is in fact nothing about herself that she does not know. I found this very surprising. Perhaps that is why she is a novelist and I am an actress. Novelists create their space and can start out omniscient, knowing every character; an actor generally is given a space to fill and a few clues — materials towards filling it — from the author. Even if you think you know yourself, when you see others who clearly think so too and, as clearly, are unaware of any of their own faults and virtues, it is hard to be so sure. People who have bad breath often don't know it — it's a nervous area. John's answer to this thorny question is a yawn. He never thinks about himself at all but turns his attention to the more arresting problems and delights of the world outside.

— you turn up for the first readthrough and after everyone has nervously gabbled, or whispered, or exploded their way through the text and the director has thanked them and pronounced himself very encouraged, he says that Wardrobe and Make-up will come round to each of us and meanwhile why doesn't the designer pass the costume designs around and we can all be looking at them. The designs pass from hand to hand and everyone admires everyone else's and examines their own anxiously — secretly pleased or dismayed; but when yours reaches you it has the name of Adrienne Corri written on it, and is clearly designed for a petite redhead. It is one thing to be grateful and flattered and available at very short notice, and to know that you were never the first choice; it is another to know who was — and that the powers that be have not yet adjusted to the change

— you turn up for the first readthrough after, once again, agreeing at very short notice to play the part; this time they have not only designed the designs — without any reference

115

to the peculiarities of your frame — they have actually gone out, bought the fabric and completed the costume for the first crucial entrance, a glamorous négligé (for the first scene on the balcony, in *Private Lives*). It is undeniably the most beautiful fabric you have ever seen, a fabulous light peach-coloured silk; it is equally undeniable that it makes you look like a barrage balloon. Since the budget cannot be stretched any further and the garment cannot be re-cut, you are obliged to make your first entrance in a bath-towel. This may express a would-be bohemian side to Amanda's character, but it is a very nerve-racking way to make your first appearance, since the towel is always in danger of falling off, and that would be too bohemian for words

233 As awful, as nerve-racking as they are, I do not like doing without a readthrough. You can eye everyone and meet almost everyone, and if you can't remember who is who, you can at least work out who among the throng is actor and who other. When I arrived at the rehearsal room for *Private Lives* they were already rehearsing, although I was on time — early in fact. We were evidently not to have a readthrough, and this left me feeling ill at ease and slightly chastised, as though I had done something wrong. When Victor and Sybil had gone through their first scene I was briefly introduced to my Elyot and we began. Which felt very bizarre.

234 I drove to nottingham via cambridge so that I could pick up Bob, who was playing Elyot, and had spent Saturday with friends. We were both nervous but excited. The road passed under a little brick bridge, and over the arch someone

had daubed in white paint the words: DON'T PRETEND. Not a very comfortable message for two thespians on their way to take up employment.

235 *things that make you appreciate men*

— a lover who takes you out to tea and arrives with a basket filled with tulips

— a bygone lover who does not forget your birthday but gets the date wrong and sends you flowers six weeks too soon; the following year more flowers arrive on the same (wrong) date, with the message, 'The annual mistake comes with perpetual love'

— a lover who presents you with a huge cardboard box halfway through lunch, in which are packed thirteen china rhinoceroses

236 MY FIRST HOUSEPLANT TAUGHT ME that although I may never be a mother I do have a maternal instinct. In the beginning I was happy just that my plant should grow and be healthy; but as time went on I found myself wanting it to flower and to be beautiful; and when it did and it was I began to want it to be not just beautiful but the most beautiful — the best. And of course, it was.

237 *unhelpful things*

— you find yourself one morning alone with the director, on the train going to rehearsals, and so you force yourself to ask for help. You have to force yourself because asking for help is something you have always found impossibly hard – a great fault. (You are worried in case when you are told – if that is possible – how to solve the problem, you still won't be able to do it.) So now you force yourself to be mature about it and say how anxious you are, how difficult the balance is to find in judging how extreme to be in this part and, in playing such a defeated character, how not to let her go under completely, or else become waspish and unsympathetic, which would have been quite wrong. You present these problems to him as best you can and he listens, frowning slightly; and when you have finished he cocks his head onto one side, grins very broadly and says with profound simplicity: 'Not to worry!' Five days before you open

– acting as assistant to a director: you agree to stand in as assistant for a friend who is not free for the first week of rehearsals; it is a play he has just directed you in, but this production is in French, in Brussels; although you are only doing the blocking* for him you discover that directors have other things to worry about than you and your performance

– an actor you are working with takes the trouble to scold you roundly for behaving as if you have come late to Drama Class and have no right to be there in the first place. 'You have every right to be there – don't forget that, ever'

– a director who occasionally reminds you of basic things that you ought not to need reminding of, such as the temperature, distances, attitudes and expectations within a scene; or he

*unless time is given to improvising, the early days of rehearsal are usually spent in 'blocking' or 'plotting' the moves

118

may simply remind you of the audience, for whom it all is — the need to be heard; things that get temporarily blurred while you are focussed on other aspects and difficulties

— a director gives you a note simply to 'say that speech again, but faster!' Sometimes a purely mechanical note, almost a musical note: faster, louder, rubato, etc., can be extraordinarily helpful and releasing, if only because your concentration suddenly goes elsewhere than on interpreting, and you don't try so hard. Speed is an interesting part of technique. One of the actors I love most, when he was being driven mad by the non-existent pace of a duologue I had, just before a scene of his, said that actors, especially younger actors, take too much time over everything. Even if you are not going to go at speed you ought to be so much in control of your material that you can if you want to. It is equally interesting when a musician abandons musical terms. Satie calls for variations such as: 'slow and sad', 'slow and grave', 'slowly and painfully', in the *Gymnopédies*; and in the *Gnossiennes*: 'with surprise', 'without pride', 'alone for a moment', 'more and more lost'. One director I know directs like a painter, calling for a different colour — something is 'too brown'; unaccustomed associations can revive you amazingly

— the advice of a friend on a first-night postcard, 'If you can't be good, be awful!'

239   *things that make your heart sink*

— even though you know it is meant as a compliment, implying that anything you do must be of interest whereas the speaker's life is very ordinary, a conversation that begins, 'And what exciting things are you up to at the moment?'

– a review of a play, that begins, 'One's heart sinks from the first moment of the play when Eleanor Bron drops an armload of cushions to stare at us aghast and go into her embarrassed hostess routine ...'

240 WHAT A CURIOUS APT DEMONSTRATION OF AFFECTION to lie at my side in the late morning, looking at the Sundays by candlelight and tactfully ignoring my tears as I read the notices.

241 A COPY OF *The Odyssey* came to my rescue: 'Explain what secret sorrow makes you weep as you listen to the tragic story of the Argives and the fall of Troy. Were not the Gods responsible for that, weaving catastrophe into the patterns of events to make a song for future generations?'

And again, Hyperion, the Sun God, speaks, "They have had the insolence to kill my cattle that gave me such joy as I climbed the sky to put the stars to flight and as I dropped from the heaven and sank once more to earth. If they do not repay me in full for my slaughtered cows, I will go down to Hades and shine among the dead." '

I had forgotten its marvellous perspective and how gripping and moving it is, and how funny. I have always preferred the Greek Gods anyway, they are so human.

242   *haunting things*

– the face of a girl struggling through ice in the Potomac River, away from the wrecked airplane; a face emptied of every sense but that struggle and its impulse, and bewilderment, and poised over absolute loss; and still more, the unidentified man, without image, legendary, who helped four others to safety, standing on the wreckage, and who had gone when rescuers came for the fifth time.

243   *things that are going*

– T.B.
– T.V.
– sea voyages
– train journeys
– typewriters
– 10p pieces
– good apples

244   *things that are gone*

– ½p pieces
– cheap paper
– cheap water
– cheap air
– telegrams
– silence
– cosy railway carriages

245   *things which are self-explanatory*

– an announcement on the train to Manchester, 'There will be a slight delay in the breakfast and buffet services. This is due to ... em ... er ... trouble in the restaurant car'

246 I WONDERED ON THE TRAIN why do so few people plant trees? It is easy to see on any journey, by train or car or bicycle, how much more delightful the roads are or estates are, where trees have been planted and had time to grow up. But you can go for miles and miles past dreary buildings and houses which would be transformed by trees, and no one bothers to plant them. Perhaps they think it is not worth the trouble, they take too long to grow and the leaves have to be raked. Or they imagine that twenty years is a long time, and they will have moved on. But apart from the shade and colour and elegance they are depriving themselves, and the future, of lungs.

247 THE SPACE, THE DOME, THE ROUNDNESS of the new theatre alarmed us all; and being surrounded, so that there would be nowhere to hide, no turning upstage to smother a cough or a corpse. Long ago, at the Establishment, I was used to being at close quarters to the audience but not, even there, to being a hologram – total exposure, all round and above, a God's-eye-view. But here, after the first few dress rehearsals and then a heart-pounding public preview came a sense of exhilaration, realising, yes, that we were as never before vulnerable but that instead of being cut off by that from our audience we came closer to them, because they unexpectedly became vulnerable with us, just as much as we were. Another revelation from this inclusion of them with us, was the sense of sharing our space with them. In Act II of *Vanya* when the storm broke far off and crept up and swept over the house and passed beyond, leaving the sound of rain dripping from the gutters, I felt that the audience was there in the room with me, hearing the dog howl and the thunder break, and experienced with me the storm and the weariness and sudden hope, and final disappointment.

248 THE LAUGHS SEEM VERY CHEAP in *Present Laughter* and so right and rich in *Private Lives*. It's not only the old tricks of using funny names, places and persons, and superior attitudes — those are the same in both. But I remember being surprised and delighted by how human Amanda and Elyot are, when I first reread it. In both plays the main characters are trying desperately to keep life at arm's length. What makes *Private Lives* so rich is that Amanda and Elyot fail to hold it off. *Present Laughter* feels barren because Garry and Joanna and Liz and even Monica, succeed only too well.

249 BEING 'OFF' LAST NIGHT was a microcosmic nightmare, a concentrate of everything that has been wrong, a kick from the donkey self into my own belly. And left me winded and very ashamed. And without a leg of self-esteeming to stand on. You really do feel winded — heart pounding, eyes starting — a sadly belated shot of adrenalin. The shock of being slapped back to life is awful. You are jerked horribly into another reality (where the reality is in fact unreality — the author's time capsule) from whatever world you have incautiously strayed into, some dream world of your own, perhaps or, in this case, the real Real World of an absorbing conversation with Rose, also waiting for her next entrance, shortly after yours. Suddenly you hear a piercing silence or — worse — awakened by the silence, you hear lines that you normally hear from another part of the stage, after you have made your exit. They have gone on, somehow, your colleagues, without you and your amusing interpolation. There can be no excuse. It is an unpardonable thing to do; understandable but unpardonable. And for some reason it seems worse in a comedy, throwing the balance so obviously. Running into Caspar at the stage door was another, better aimed, more salutary helping kick; he gave me a note that

actually confirmed the creeping faults of the performance: 'knowingness' – commenting on the lines instead of saying them. I had thought at least I knew what I was doing here – and was not even right about that one, elementary ... In the face of all this crumbling I feel quite jolly. Perhaps a fall comes before getting up again.

250 *things that are born of good intentions but stand small chance of succeeding*

– an actor who has been in a famous production of the play you are doing, is in town to do a television play. He sends invitations to some but not all of the company to dine with him after the evening's performance, which he will attend. Although it is unreasonable to expect him to invite the entire company you are depressed for those who have been left out; nor can you imagine that he or any other actor could possibly have been better in his role than your actor, and you feel as proud of your production and as possessive of the play as he once did, and does still. He is gracious and hospitable but inevitably, indefinably, indelibly conveys the impression that your interpretation of the play is inferior to that great one years ago. He says kind things, but you are left with an empty feeling

– friends whom you have not seen for a long time invite you to dinner; one of the guests is a famous photographer who is visiting England on a tour to find subjects of a book of the World's Most Beautiful Women. You suspect that your kind hosts hoped you might take his fancy, but the photographer does not click

– a friend advises you, when you have had a bad audience – an unreceptive matinée perhaps – to think to yourself that there is almost certainly one person out there who is appreciating the show; awareness of that one person should concentrate and refresh your performance. This advice reminds you of King Solomon's famous ring, devised by his wise counsellors to cure his melancholy. When he felt sad he was to look at this ring with its inscription, 'This too will pass'; but you know that your eye would light on it at some moment when you were feeling really happy. In the same way at a performance which is going wonderfully well, roars of laughter, high attention, bated breath, it always crosses your mind that somewhere out there there is one person who is hating every second

– the flat you have rented in Bristol has a fireplace, and when you go for a walk on the Downs you decide to collect some kindling for a fire; you feel a little self-conscious at first; then you find that you are talking, muttering to yourself as you go. This has the strange effect of making you feel that you are not alone – shutting out other people. It also makes you feel less conspicuous, though it probably makes you more so

– you wake from a dream which you cannot recall exactly, but as you try to bring it back you find that you do know that one person in it was someone you like or dislike, or feel warmly towards, or threatened by; for the moment all you can remember is a kind of flavour that person has for you. When, suddenly, you do remember who it is, it is sometimes quite surprising to discover that that is what you feel towards them. This can happen in an everyday way – just before you actually remember someone's name you remember their flavour, an emotional colour

– in another variation you are arranging to meet somewhere with a friend, but you are reluctant to go as far afield as they are suggesting; you realise that you have a scale of levels for putting yourself out, and this friend is slipping down it

— you find yourself telling a man that you are afraid of boring him; later you realise that the reverse is also true, or perhaps only the reverse is true; you wonder how many such emotions are reversible

— you have had a drink with an acquaintance after the show. He offers to see you safely back to the flat you have rented. You remember that you left it in a total panic, because an enormous, a giant, bug — either a June bug or a Kafka-sized cockroach — had appeared in the tiny bathroom, buzzing and flapping about, rattling the shower curtain, far more frightened than you, no doubt ... You are terrified to go into the bathroom and gratefully accept your amused and fearless escort's offer to get rid of the thing for you. In the bathroom there is no sign of it at all. Your escort is delighted that your pudeur should have driven you to this quaint, unnecessary ruse to lure him in. Your protestations are of little avail. But eventually you persuade him to leave. Later in the bathroom when you tug at the lavatory roll, the great bug, which has been waiting there, falls onto your knees

— your lover turns up at your flat one night during your last week of filming; you are just about to go to bed, anxiously hoping for a good night's sleep, because next day you have a difficult, emotional scene; you tell him he must leave, but he does not take you seriously; you get more and more angry at this simultaneous invasion and dismissal and by the time you do manage to push his protesting form out of the door and into the lift, you are in a nervous rage, convinced that now you will not sleep a wink. Infuriated by the prospect of a sleepless night when you need all your energy and wits about you, you rush to the window at the front, pick up a flowerpot — full of earth waiting for seedlings — open the window and wait until you hear the street door open downstairs. The balustrade under your window means you can't see the street and have to judge as best you can the moment when the pot should fall just behind him and give him a nasty shock. It also obliges you to heave the thing quite far out. It is you who gets the shock: there is no sound of it landing. You realise that you were just too late getting to the window, because suddenly you see him disappearing down the street. The fall of your flowerpot must have been interrupted by someone else. You rush downstairs in your dressing-gown to see whom you have murdered. Earth and bits of flowerpot are scattered wide. There is no one in sight

(You sleep very well. The scene next day is about a woman having a row with her estranged husband and trying to make him leave her flat ...)

253 NOW THAT PLASTIC FLOWERS AND PLANTS are made to look so lifelike, Claus asked me why do I bother with my windowsill, which is sometimes pretty and sometimes pathetic; straggling and messy and needing constant attention? Exactly, I said. The thing about plastic or silk flowers is that they have no poignancy because they cannot die. Real flowers need us. The most we can do for plastic flowers is to dust them occasionally.

254 WHEN YOUR LOVER ASKS, 'What would you say to Perth, Australia?' what do you answer? Well, to him, say, 'It's

supposed to be lovely.' To yourself next day, 'Goodbye, John.' Why go thousands of miles – assuming he were to ask – when you can suffer at home in the comfort of your garden swing? If we haven't done it here how much less likely there. All the clues are negative.

255 FOR A LONG TIME I AVOIDED doing a one-woman show. I had always had a feeling about them that they were probably some kind of ego trip for the actor; that his or her intention was of the 'Look at Me, wonderful Me!' sort, a difficult side of show business, because it introduces Personality. When it works it can be marvellous, depending on the performer – like the nursery rhyme, 'When she was good she was very very good, but when she was bad she was horrid.'

But I decided that the time had come to leave the reading aloud of chosen verses and try to assemble and shape an evening that I would perform entirely from memory, and I agreed to do a show for a Literary Festival. After one brief technical run in the afternoon, with rudimentary lighting and props, I was almost but not quite prepared for the terror of that first performance. I had supposed, since in performing a play with other actors you feel a sense of responsibility to your colleagues and a strong wish not to let them down, that as a solo performer you would feel your responsibility to be to yourself – a desire not to let yourself down. But as I stepped onto the stage I realised abruptly that this was not the case at all, and that my sole responsibility was to the audience. I must not let them down or abandon them. They must not for a moment feel nervous about me or for me. Whether they liked me or the show was immaterial: their minds must be untroubled by my fear, so that they could be at liberty to like or loathe.

This very powerful lesson now seems an obvious one and of course in any play your responsibility is to your audience and to your author, as well as to your fellow actors — you yourself are of small consequence; but at the time this obvious truth was a revelation and a great release. The rewards of such an evening are unique, of very direct, reciprocated communication.

256 IT IS BAD ENOUGH TO HAVE A LOVER who cannot drive; if in addition he is unable to read a map, then in every sense you are on the wrong track.

257   *maddening things*

— you are setting out — rather later than you had planned — to drive to the next stop on your tour. Since you have been staying in a flat and had a kitchen and have left-over provisions, and since you have had a very late breakfast, and since the weather continues wonderfully fine and fresh, you both agree that it would be delightful to have a picnic on the way rather than be forced to have lunch at a pub before you are really hungry. You set out in high spirits because you know that you are going to drive through the most beautiful countryside, from Chester down through the Cotswolds. Your lover, who is normally the worst navigator in the world, has studied the map and planned a most delightful route, and you drive happily for over an hour. At Worcester he suggests a small detour to see the great Cathedral, which is most impressive and you admire the inside, though the hideous modern precinct which faces it across the roundabout is depressing. You have a cup of tea in the café run by the Friends of the Cathedral while he looks for the crypt. It is quite surprising to find that you have spent well over an hour there and you decide that you will stop for lunch as soon as you see a good place. The car has become very hot and, though it will cool down once you are underway, you are afraid that certain perishable things, like the cheese and cream, may have suffered.

It takes quite a long time to find your way out of the city and even once you have, the route seems now more difficult to follow. The navigation has definitely gone off. Moreover the road is no longer as pretty and there are fewer trees — only occasionally at the side of fields. You suggest stopping for lunch under one of these trees but your proposal is greeted with horror. He says that it would be rude to go onto the farmer's land to eat your lunch without permission. He objects to the village green in the next village, with its convenient bench, because the green belongs to the villagers, who don't want their Sunday spoiled by having to watch us eating our lunch on their green. He rejects another shady spot, on the edge of a wood, because there is another car there and people can be glimpsed through the trees. He declines to stop at the side of the road because it is the side of the road. You begin to suspect him of secretly reading *The Taming of the Shrew*.

Finally, as you drive through Evesham you take a wrong turning which leads you along one bank of the river. This is a public park planted with trees and flowers, shady and cool, with water flowing and not too many people. You decide to stop no matter what and leave him in the car if need be. You cannot find a parking space. You drive on.

It is getting on for six when at last, still lunchless, you reach your destination. Before you go to your hotel you drive round the town where you find a newly built Sports Centre near a murky bit of river that is full of beer cans and empty crisp packets, with a few trees and two rusty green bridges. There is plenty of parking space. Here, under one of the trees, you swallow the crushed and melting remains from your basket, battling with wasps

– it is Christmas time and your lover has, as usual, skived off – an abrupt disappearance and no clue to his whereabouts or to when you may see each other again. You decide that there is no sense in it, it's not balanced by anything. Silver apples and agate hearts and antique velvet bonnets and china rhinos are not enough; the guts still ache, the shock still shakes, the bruises last a long time. You resolve that this was the last time; and for a little while you are so full of your hurt that you really believe it

– making the mistake of treating a newspaper interviewer like a real person; on the radio, or on the television, people can hear or see what you intend, but in print even a verbatim quotation can seem to mean the opposite of what you said

– at school, at fourteen, a girl considers you and your friends to be very fast, minces up to you all in the dinner-hour, sniggering, and says, pursing her mouth up, 'I bet you're talking about *rude* things.' When you ask her what does she mean by rude things, she goes purple, stands on one leg, waggling the other, and finally explodes, 'Boys!'

– you are at the last night party for *The Cherry Orchard*. There is a good feeling that the production had worked very well and the new theatre at the Riverside may rise from the dust and rubble, towards some sort of glory. You are feeling fine since, although Carlotta is an awful part to play, so depressing, with all those one-liners and on top of that, nerve-racking conjuring tricks, everyone has said nice things, and you are proud to have been a part of the company. An actor comes up to you whom you have met, never worked with, a passing acquaintance. He does say 'Hello' but then immediately, 'Is it true you had an affair with Paul McCartney?' You are too flabbergasted to dredge up, let alone invent any countering riposte to hurl at him from his none too inspiring past. Perhaps he is one of those people who pride themselves on their bluntness. Afterwards you remember that he lives with or is married to the rawboned redhead from the *Pippin* audition, and that makes sense

260 I CANNOT WAIT TO SEE THE PIGS AGAIN this year, and the Shire Horses, although I resisted mightily the idea of the Royal Show and was so reluctant to go last time, the first time. Rows of pens in rough dark wood, set back to back in lines across the field; sows and sheep stewing in the heat — incredible panting of the sheep's sides, as if each were in a seizure of panic, a death throe, lying gasping with half-closed eyes. The pigs are amazingly hairy, sparse coarse hair, black or pale patches that produce great blotched markings seen from a distance; or pale hair over the aggressively pink skin — that human look. The pale lashes make their eyes look like those of dozy statesmen, whereas on the men they make for sinister inhuman figures. The people are casual, rightful, in jeans and wellingtons and tweed jackets, moving to fill buckets and push the animals aside without respect, but sometimes with affection. This pen has rapidly become base; home, familiar for three days. Worlds away from them the visitors in laced suede shoes or sandals and summer dresses and sunglasses, who stroll through peeping and exclaiming, as if they had never seen a first-class swayback before.

– you are angry because another actor is deliberately trying to corpse you by not giving you your cue in the usual way; it is not until you reach your dressing-room that you realise that on the contrary you had dried, and it was you who had utterly failed to give him his cue

– you have decided that only a system using coloured paper clips can bring urgently needed order into your writings; after vainly trying four stationers the fifth produces the goods; as you are about to pay for them you notice that they are made in South Africa; you buy them anyway

– finding letters asking for a photo, with s.a.e., a year, two years, ten years later; especially if the letter is written in an old, shaky hand

– treating a young, very inexperienced journalist, who is trying to interview you, with gratuitous unpleasantness

– in your terror on the first night, confused by two identical entrances and the afternoon's dress rehearsal, you cut – from the end of Act I to Act III, eliminating entirely two intervals and the whole of Act II. Afterwards your director comments drily, 'It's quite a good cut, actually . . .'

263 THE BIRDS MUST HAVE SEVERAL FEEDING GROUNDS and visit them in order, to check developments. Ours was soon established. At first there was never a sign of a bird until the food was down; after a few weeks there were frequent complaints from both pigeons and sparrows – though never from the two together – if the supply were late for some reason. They would wait on the fence and watch, as little lumps of bread pattered down on to the stone. At the sound of the window's closing they would fly away a short way, rising into the air and flying to a further fence or a high window-sill. A few minutes later they would be on the ground, on the fence, shooting up and down, up and down again, pecking and flying and wiping their beaks on the fence, jerking their heads from side to side, hopping, flying down again for more. The food goes very quickly.

264 YESTERDAY I WENT DOWN TO JOHN LEWIS to see what they have in the way of furnishing fabric. I crossed Wigmore Street behind three little girls with satchels who were discussing classes and marks, how long they spend on one vocab – a fortnight now instead of a week. 'What did you get?'

'Ten.'

'Ten mistakes?'

'No! Ten right.'

The questioner looked anxious, as if ten mistakes was too many, but ten right was far too many. She was the only one who betrayed any sense that someone was close behind them, me, and might be overhearing their talk. As we were waiting for the next traffic light to change, a blonde woman, not young, rather well-groomed, with a kind face, darted up to me and said, 'Don't look so unhappy. You're too beautiful to be unhappy,' and was gone. It was not an order, it was a request, almost a plea. The little girls stared for a moment, the lights changed and we all moved on.

Beauty, we are reminded often enough, is in the eye of the beholder, but I was curious and looked in the mirror on the way to the escalator. What I saw was indeed sad and sorry enough, but more sullen than unhappy – the snooty look that always had me lining the wall at dances in my teens; and haggard. Enough people have told me that I am beautiful for me to have accepted the possibility, certainly when photographed in the right light and mood; but I have seen too many of the wrong shots to be convinced or confident. Fortunately, for an actress a mobility between ugliness and beauty is supposed to be a greater asset than straightforward loveliness.

And yet I know that I have been lying to myself at least a little by my reaction to time passing, the crumpling skin, the greying hair – if I thought there was nothing there what do I fear to lose? Your eyes begin to look smaller as if you have

136

been crying. Is that what she saw and mistook for sadness? Or did she recognise me and think that I should have been more beautiful than that?

265 NOBLESSE OBLIGE: IF YOU ARE PRIVILEGED look as if it's worth it. If you are in a chauffeur-driven limousine learn to smile. Wealth, fame and beauty really are worth having: only if you have them can you know for sure, beyond all doubt, that finally it is all up to you – an end to hankering.

As Ludwig of Bavaria instructed his servants, 'Remind me to look happier tomorrow.'

266 I ASKED A FRIEND IF HE WAS HAPPY rehearsing for a new play. He said he didn't mind not liking the play, but that so far he found his fellow-actors uncongenial too. 'Apart from anything else they are very bitchy,' he said, and reported a strange coffee-break conversation. They were talking about a well-known actress and one of the company dismissed her, saying, 'Her trouble is that she thinks she's the most beautiful woman in the world.'

'Oh,' said one of the actresses, 'You mean like Eleanor Bron?'

More astonishing than this remark was my friend's noble reply, 'But Eleanor Bron *is* the most beautiful woman in the world.'

This statement was greeted with a stunned silence.

Since he told me this story I look in the mirror with renewed hope, with curiosity, and with amazement that anyone could imagine that someone who confronts this face before breakfast should hang on to such an odd idea of Beauty. The most arrogant woman in the world, possibly – but even then I can think of other candidates.

267 PEOPLE WERE ACTUALLY QUEUING for returns for the last performances of my one-woman show and of course I was feeling pleased and happy that it had gone down so well. Lovely unexpected people turned up out of the blue. On the last night lots of friends and some total strangers came round and my dressing-room was buzzing with heady praise and congratulations, when suddenly into the room erupted an old Bristol friend, an actor, frowning, red-faced, and vehement. He leapt up and down, booming in his voice like thunder: 'You *must* not do it, Eleanor! You must not *do* it!'

The room stopped dead. Did he mean the whole show? Were they all standing accused as liars? What he was so angry about was my introduction – talking to the audience before I start the show proper. What I *must* not *do*, was apologise. I know what he means. But how hard to change.

268 MY SECOND ATTEMPT AT *Tristan* was almost redeemed by Alberto Remedios with his extraordinary tenderness and humanity; but it still seemed endless. In spite of all his lushness and emotion Wagner feels inhuman – too much Übermensch and not enough Mensch. He is finally just not Jewish enough. Mahler is too Jewish; Bartók is just right.

269 GREAT MUSIC CAN DO A LOT OF HARM if it's not used carefully. It can show up a play or film and reduce where it is meant to enhance. *Travesties* suffered from its Beethoven

Sonata — though at least it didn't devour the Sonata the way *Elvira Madigan* devoured its Mozart Piano Concerto, so that it is only just beginning to reconstitute itself for me again. But sometimes, usually when the music, heard by one of the characters, is accompanied by the revelation of something buried (a memory or a feeling recovered), it can be unbelievably powerful. Mozart again, in the film *Une Aussi Longue Absence*, or the Beethoven Violin Concerto in *Duet for One*. Or it can be a revelation, quite apart from anything, an illumination, mysterious: Cocteau's use of the Bach/Vivaldi in *Les Enfants terribles*; Kubrick's double Strauss — the Blue Danube and Zarathustra, in *2001*; Herzog's Pachelbel Canon, in *The Enigma of Kaspar Hauser*.

270   *dazzling things*

— the Juggler at the Circus Championships, juggling first with cigar boxes, then with top hats; there seemed to be a circle of shining hats around his body as if he had stopped time and we were looking at a slow-motion photograph

— at Mere in Wiltshire, the hang-glider rising higher and higher, disappearing beyond our ability to focus on such a tiny speck; the hang-gliders with motors are very intrusive and seem pointless; someone described them as 'flying lawnmowers'

— the sound of a matinée audience before a Christmas pantomime

271 TWICE DAILY IS CRUEL even if it is only for six weeks. I don't know how anyone survives doing the full panto season — though perhaps a decent wage might help. On the

139

telephone describing to my father my state of fatigue: how I crawl home after midnight, have a bowl of John's vegetable soup and go straight to bed; wake up aching (most of us have caught or are fending the company flu), have time for a few chores before setting off to the theatre again to make up, do the show, snatch a nap if I can in the concrete cell which is our dressing-room, do the show again, drink a quick drink, and home; 'I'm *exhausted*,' I moan, 'absolutely worn out!'

My father says, 'That's what work is like, Eleanor.'

— soup, mugs of tea, hot water bottles, perfume, a beautiful Christmas garment knitted by a friend

— strangers: a bus-driver who is just about to start on his route leaps out of his cab to tell you how marvellous he thought you and the play were on T.V. last night; a message on your answering machine, in answer to yours — that you have gone to the dentist — 'Well, actually it's a wrong number. I don't know you but I just hung on to say that I hope you didn't have too bad a time at the dentist and are feeling O.K.'

273 DAVID SENT ME THE FOLLOWING CUTTING, from the Chinese publication *Scientia Sinica*:

CORRECTION
In article 'Devote Every Effort to Running Successfully Socialist Research Institutes of Science' (Sci. Sin. Vol XIX No. 5), 'the arch unrepentant capitalist-roader in the party, Teng Hsaio-ping' should read 'Teng Hsaio-ping'.

274 IN THE KENNELS THE GUN DOGS LEAPT FORWARD to greet us with a great clamour of enthusiasm, yelping and pushing and wagging their tails. One dog remained behind, apart and unlike, cringing back and trembling all over. He had been, still was, a marvellous gun-dog; but one day while out hunting, he had been accidentally shot. It was a punishment that he could not understand. He knew that to have been punished he must have done something wrong, but he could not grasp what or why. His nerves as well as his body had been shattered, but only his body had recovered.

275   *things that go on for a long time*

– a birthday present of a travelling water-colour box, made of brass. It measures 3 × 5 inches and is hinged. The cover that holds together the two halves removes to contain water, which is carried within one of the halves; the other holds twelve colours and a folding paintbrush. There are white enamel palettes which fold open for mixing the paints

276 I MOVED A WHOLE HILL YESTERDAY with a slip of the brush, translating it to fiction; but left an awkward gap where the trees should reach to, so that they practically obliterated that red-brown patch of ploughed land. I shall have to invent some hedges and walls and put in a few more brushes to fill the blank. Or should I somehow shove the bank of trees up higher so that their tops are where they ought to be, in spite of the banished hillock? No one will mind if I lie about the landscape, as long as it looks possible. So it ought to be possible to create life out of fragments and memories and phrases, that will bear some resemblance to something, someone, and be believable. What if the resemblance is too much?

277 THIS PROCESS OF LEARNING A NEW SKILL too often teaches me more about myself than about the skill – among other things, my lack of staying power. While I was learning to drive I noted a tendency, if anybody honked, to assume they were honking at me. While I was learning to type I found a tendency to go wrong if I thought the person next to me was going wrong, and to blame the racket of the machines, or the machines themselves. Learning to paint has been more interesting. Literalness presents itself as one besetting sin. Where to end the picture, the edges, has not been hard to decide (right or wrong); but within the frame I cannot stop myself yet from attempting every wrinkle on the counterpane, every knob on the radio, every twig on the tree. Choice raises its head here as in all forms of art, but I have no instinct at all for selection in this one. Perhaps that can be acquired. But can I do anything about the other trait, too obvious to ignore: meanness? Counting the cost has been much to the fore. I guess that to be a painter you have to be a lavisher, a waster, to have a generous nature; the ability to squander in search. Whereas I, once I have mixed a colour, feel under the inaesthetic obligation to use it all up – I am so aware of how much each of those tiny little blocks costs. And if one colour starts to get more used up than the others – bye bye Truth!

(I am writing these words on the back of old television scripts ...)

278   *things you wish you had done*

– when a bully of a film director picked needlessly on an elderly actress, humiliating her in front of the whole unit, one of the leading actors quietly returned to his caravan and refused to go back on the location until the director apologised. The director duly came to the caravan to apologise but the actor said no, he must apologise to the actress, and

142

in front of the unit. Only when this had been done would he agree to carry on filming

— when, in an improvisation workshop, a seriously experimental director gave his company five minutes, so that they could each think up something to surprise him, one actress went home

— directors who cannot admit to any vulnerability but bolster their shaky egos by exposing the most vulnerable members of the cast; if they are asked for help they grin and refuse any responsibility or involvement, saying, 'Find it! Find it!' — as if they have the answer but won't tell

280 WHEN MARIAN WAS WAITING TO GO ON for her first, extremely difficult, entrance in Act I, the director came rushing up to her. She thought he must have some important note he had forgotten to give her on the previous evening; but he stuck his head under the brim of her great hat and said urgently, close into her ear, 'Come to bed with me, come to bed with me, come to bed with me!'

281 SHAW AGAIN. I MISS EMOTIONAL LOGIC when I play in Shaw. He is always so busy doing his astounding mental somersaults and all kinds of dizzying volte-faces, but the hearts of his characters never seem to have 'their reasons which reason does not understand'. Someone the other day said that in Shaw and in Coward people too often make the mistake of casting actors who can play intelligence, wit,

sophistication, coolness, ego and so on; but in fact all that is already supplied in bulk by both authors and it is far more needful to cast actors who have warmth.

– a winter dream: you wake up on a cold day, snug in bed; miraculously, you rise – without effort or urging – and wash and dress and find yourself quite painlessly ready for breakfast and the day. Then you really wake up and realise that it was only a dream and now you must drag yourself from the warmth and start the whole business all over again

– an older actress whom you admire is at a fund-raising dinner and makes a great point of asking to be introduced to you, calling you a splendid creature and demanding to know why you are not playing the great classic roles. 'When are we going to see your "Hedda"?' She is charmed and excited to hear that your Hedda has already been seen, at Worthing, and full of kindness and endearing flatteries. Some time later, when you are playing one of the great roles, you learn that she is coming to a matinée. You hope that she may come backstage afterwards but she does not. You feel that you have failed

– you visit a schoolfriend whom you have not seen for many years; her father has died suddenly and all her family is gathered; in the kitchen you are chatting with her when her husband comes in and announces, addressing you, 'I've got a bone to pick with you.' He then proceeds to take you to task because some years before you had refused to commère a Charity show which was to raise money for Jewish refugees of the Six Day War. The reason you refused was that the idea of discriminating between refugees seemed appalling, especially if you are Jewish – to be a refugee is terrible whatever your nationality or religion; you told the organiser that you would be glad to take part if the money were to go to Jewish *and* Arab refugees, and it seems that this has shocked the Jewish community to its core. The kitchen recriminations coming out of left field leave you feeling pretty shaky; and nothing is improved when you tell the story to your parents expecting their sympathy, and they are equally shocked by your naïve views

– you scan the T.V. columns to see what sort of preview the critics have given the play that is going out that night – the first time you have been cast in a straight drama on T.V. The play has been chosen 'Pick of the Day' and you read eagerly. Yes, it is very favourable about the play – but does it really mean to single out your 'virtuous performance'?

283 THE FESTIVAL AT MONTEPULCIANO is not a festival according to the organisers, but a 'workshop', trying to 'counteract the centralisation of artistic activity in the larger conurbations of Italy, by bringing such events out to the more culturally underdeveloped communities ...', in this case a relatively poor farming region whose main product is a red wine called Vino Nobile. Whatever it is, festival or workshop, Montepulciano is a glorious place for it, once you get there. After six or seven years the local inhabitants have stopped resisting and come to accept, perhaps even enjoy, the sudden summer influx of arty folk, and the arty folk are certainly rapturous about Montepulciano. Apparently it is not alone among small Tuscany hill towns in having its own theatre – like the one in *Where Angels Fear to Tread*. The theatre here is small but quite grand, and very beautiful, with tiers of seats in the old horseshoe shape. Above the entrance outside, some words of their sixteenth-century poet struck a bond with me

across the years, 'My best order is to be in the state of confusion.'

284 Up very early and reluctantly, obeying last night's resolution, we left the white chamber and passed down the hotel staircase, which was like passing through a work of art. Not simply because the whiteness drained the colour from the stones, or because of the arched walls and unexpected turns, but the coolness – that particular appeal to the senses had a shock of mastery about it; and later in the day, when outside was burning, of miracle.

We had the town to ourselves. Except, as we climbed the dark-grey stones, increasingly there were sweepers, sweeping with long strokes, taking advantage of the early freshness, or moonlighting perhaps, in the morning: get this job done and on to another, and another after that.

We climbed up past the fortress and the same view, a little lower, that I had seen at evening from the terrace, spread out before us. Clearer, sharper, and brighter; shadows not so apparent, falling the other way. There was no more of last night's milkiness, tell-tale cypress trees and cigar-shaped poplars less mysterious at this time of day. We walked on, pleased with ourselves as much as with what we saw, for being up early, for being together. At a gateway we examined the great gear that once would have lowered the barrier to the city walls. Above the wall, across the arch of the city entrance, was a little house built, one storey only – an elevated bungalow. Wonderful to live there and look out: inward on the city down from above at who comes who goes; and outward in the evening, at the milky world, roads and hills and other cities on other hills. And profusions of plants trailing, geraniums, bougainvillaea, high up in a high city.

285 INSIDE THE THEATRE the audience managed to stay alive in spite of the sweltering heat. (Even in Italy it was proclaimed a heat wave.) The air tried to attach itself to you. I kept it at bay with my fan until the ballet was done (ballet in this heat!) and it was time for *Façade*. I stepped on to the stage, and I was alright until I got through my first piece, 'En Famille', and sat down. Immediately I broke into streams of sweat. My hair clung to the back of my neck, my back trickled, flowed. I tried to mop discreetly with a tissue. I was grateful at least that I was wearing something loose – my Indian two-piece in red muslin. The smocky top-half reaches to my knees and touches me not at all. I was even more grateful for that when we took our calls at last and above the hubbub of generous applause and shouts of 'Brava! Bravo!' I distinctly heard one voice shouting, 'Trousers! Trousers!' I thought it must be John, but he denies it utterly. And yet as I went off into the wings I noticed a pleasing absence of sensation around my waist. It took a moment to realise that my trousers were indeed drifting downwards, wrinkling about my ankles with a view to settling there. My next bows must have looked oddly nonchalant, shuffling on slowly, with one hand behind my back, clutching a fistful of red cheesecloth.

286   *surprising things*

– the heat generated by a mosquito bite that has swollen overnight

287 KIERKEGAARD IS VERY ENDEARING, with his wonderfully sympathetic view of actresses:

I suppose that when most people think of an actress of the first rank they imagine her condition in life to be so enchanting that they generally quite forget its thorny side: the incredibly many trivialities and all the unfairness or misunderstanding, just at the critical moment, that an actress may have to contend with ...

288 *dreadfully disappointing things*

— your agent calls to tell you he has made an appointment for you to see Fellini; next day he calls to tell you that it has been cancelled

289 *things which excite comment, sometimes with a flavour of disapprobation, because although they have nothing to do with morals they depart from some unspoken norm, and make you seem slightly eccentric, or 'camp' (even though some of them, over the years, have become almost modish), but which all came about initially for perfectly good reasons*

— wearing more than three chains or necklaces round your neck

— having a garden swing in your living-room instead of a sofa

— riding a bicycle in London

— leaving the price tag on things around the house: lamps, cushions, rugs, etc.

— not hanging pictures, leaving them around the skirting

— having your bed on the bias instead of parallel to, or against a wall

– filling a kettle through its spout

– eating the crusts of bread and leaving the middle

– on the radio in Chicago, a commercial for Faith: 'Faith makes you feel good. Nurture and protect it (in your Church or Synagogue)'

– in a trial, the defence calls an expert witness to give an opinion on the course of action taken by one of the defendants; the judge acknowledges that the witness is impressive but dismisses her evidence because 'she is too much of a perfectionist'

– you are appearing in a Christmas show, a limited West End run at West End prices. The show consists of the actors sitting on tall stools and getting up from time to time to recite or sing and do a little gentle choreography, with slides and lighting effects – not as exhausting as a pantomime but taxing, because the cast is on stage throughout and it is too easy to drift off into a dream. One evening at the stage door a woman tells you, eyes aglow, that it was the best thing she has seen in the theatre all year. You cannot disguise your horror, nor she her horror at your horror; but what a terrible thing if this confection really were the best entertainment the West End has offered for the last twelve months

291 HOW VULNERABLE PEOPLE CAN SEEM, sitting in a theatre. Being on stage all evening as yourself, watching them, is full of lessons and interest. You form relationships with them, of pure supposition. Defensive attitudes they take up, the men more than the women, protecting themselves against assault,

149

sexual or otherwise. They often look quite helpless. And others bring so much and offer with great openness and receive hugely and swiftly. There was a girl with three children, and so much delight pouring out of her. Something I could cultivate – it is rarely that expression that I take to the theatre. Or anywhere. Lovely to see. Nor do all children have it.

292 ONE OF THE SONGS STRUCK ME one evening, suddenly, as being exceptionally silly, and once I had this view it began to seem, every time, interminable, and I dreaded every night the endless moment when I should have to sit through it. Then I started to notice what the double bass was doing, under the melody, playing a very gentle harmony that was so lovely that I began to listen for it and then to look forward to it and to delight in it so much that it became the only moment of the evening for me. When it was over my disappointment was acute and the rest of the performance seemed emptier than ever.

293 I WATCHED A YOUNG MAN DURING THE DUET this evening, in the front row of the stalls with glasses and a Thermos flask. He unscrewed the cup from the Thermos and put it on his lap. Then he unscrewed the stopper and searched for a place to rest it so that he could pour out. By this time the song was in full flow and they had started to dance, but he barely glanced up at the stage. He balanced the stopper next to the cup, poured his coffee carefully, spilling nothing, put back the stopper and returned the Thermos with one hand, circumspectly, to some container on the floor at his feet. He then immediately extracted a packet from the container, took

150

a sandwich from the packet, unwrapping it with one hand, his coffee still in the other, held the sandwich up to the light of the stage to see whether it was egg or cucumber or jam, put it on his lap, took up the packet again and returned it to the container, and finally picked up his sandwich and sat with sandwiches and coffee ready to eat. Lucky man.

294 THE LAST NIGHT WITH WILD APPLAUSE and encores filled me with gloom. I hate encores anyway, unless you can offer something new instead of merely repeating what you have just done. So I am torn between dread of being called on and humiliation of not. Nose anyway not just out of joint but severely broken by end of run.

295   *difficult things*

— ignoring a wonderful notice from a critic whom you normally dismiss

— doing reaction shots (as Mary, Mother of Jesus) to a Crucifixion which was filmed three days before you arrived

296 WE HAD THE BUS TO OURSELVES almost all the way to Exmouth, sun and clouds over bare fields. I was going on about the sensation during the last few years of having a D & C of the brain, so literally empty-headed, as if my mind had been scraped of all content. The mindlessness of entertaining anyone to such talk as we bowled through pretty villages and country lanes, and my insistence on persevering with this topic did seem to bear out what I was saying.

151

297 TODAY THE NEW VENTURE, my exercise class, a cliff-hanger: would I manage to find a way to set out just too late to make it worthwhile going? I lay down on the swing and plunged into unconsciousness — but woke up again in good time. I gathered my things and got there feeling brave and with ten minutes to spare; plenty of time to join up. Not allowing myself to be put off by the aura of fitness and purpose, the sight of bronzed young men lounging in the reception area, I pursued my own purpose and asked about membership. A green card handed to me required among other things my age and telephone number. I flinched and went on flinching quietly. Observing this the girl said kindly why didn't I fill it in later. I was shown to the changing room, where there were three lissom bronzed young women in bandanas and legwarmers and gleaming satin summer leotards in leopard prints. I flinched again more severely and retreated to the lavatory; reasoned with myself, as if I were a grown-up person, tried to shame myself into going on with it all, tried to get into my footless black tights, so terribly square; but it was too sticky and hot to manage to pull them much beyond my calf. My bare foot on the floor reminded me too that I had no jazz shoes — surely a *sine qua non*. The last straw. I baulked and finally relinquished — just remembering to flush the lavatory, my alibi, before I left the cubicle, and hurried out, out of the changing-room, out of the building; grateful that the receptionist was not at her post. So — another door closed. How shall I ever flex myself again? Buy the Jane Fonda book to add to all those others? Yoga, Mensendieck, Alexander, Canadian Air Force, aerobics, Berk, Mendau ... Get up early and walk round the Park.

298 I HAVE NEVER HEARD SO MUCH ILL SPOKEN of one actor. He seems to have managed to put up every single back in

152

the studio. Not just the usual areas of potenial altercation: producer, director, assistants, wardrobe, make-up, etc.; but stand-in as well, grips, gaffers, cameraman, focus-puller — not one person has a good word to say for him. William, the driver, who gets on with everyone, is the only one who has personally no evil story to report; but even he, when I mentioned the universal loathing that had been aroused, had been witness to one manifestation of it. He had driven the man back to Claridges, where he was staying. It was a filthy night, a ceaseless downpour from open heavens. As the car drew up in front of the hotel the doorman stepped forward, his huge umbrella at the ready; but when he saw who the passenger was, he turned his back, closed the umbrella and walked away.

299 WE WERE TALKING ABOUT AMBITION AND AMBITIONS. Andrew said his only ambition was to have delusions of grandeur.

300 MY TYPEWRITER AND I DO NOT ALWAYS SEE i to i, but today it referred to Mrs Thatcher's 'unfluence' ...

301   *things that seem right*

— your local bookshop ranges its paperbacks around the walls in the basement with a sign above each stack of shelves: FICTION, BIOGRAPHY, TRAVEL, HUMOUR, etc. Outsize books are laid flat along the base of the stacks. You note that *The British Army in the Falklands* has been placed under CRIME.

– religious convictions

– the Law: lawyers and judges

– thunder

– the baying of an audience before a charity show in which the Monty Python team is appearing

– to wake up to the Waltz from Berlioz's *Symphonie fantastique*

– The London Library: the red carpets and polished wood, clanging footsteps of browsers in the stacks and on the metal walkways, even the continuous buzz of the fluorescent lights there. Great peace – only once disturbed by Magooley coming up behind me in the Reading Room and saying in tones of utter astonishment, 'What on earth are *you* doing here?'

– going to sleep

– going to sleep to the sound of someone in another room playing a Chopin Waltz

304 WHEN I TOLD JOHN THAT I HAD FOUND something in Bristol that would delight me but not him, he didn't need his three guesses but got it in one. 'It must be the largest wholemeal loaf in the world.' But even he would love that bakery: white loaves, french, cottage, tin, danish, as well as black, harvest and overnight, rye and sourdough and sesame; a wonderful humming place with a huge space behind the counter with to-ing and fro-ing of loaded trays and great

busyness and chatter between the women in their overalls as they serve crowds of customers – a couple of croissants or a polythene sack full of rolls.

– you intend going straight past the bear enclosure at Clifton Zoo because you do not like bears – they enjoy a far too flattering image. In reality they are not cuddly at all but among the fiercest and beastliest of animals and the most likely to attack without provocation. The shaggy pelt does not hide fat content, but a lean and hungry belly, and their padded paws have long claws that can rip you open at one swipe. They have long mean muzzles and cruel eyes. You had no intention of visiting them but you are arrested by the sight of one of the three polar bears. The enclosure is roomy and cragged with artificial peaks, and two of the bears are down below, one lounging and one wandering. But this third, the largest bear, is all alone on a tiny crag-top, a platform not much more than two yards square, and on this tiny island he never stops moving, backward and forward, one step two steps forward, one step two steps back, front legs forward back legs forward, back legs backward front legs backward. And again. One visitor already there remarks that he has been performing this ritual ever since she arrived, twenty minutes before; and when you go back, an hour later, out of curiosity, he is still lost in his endless basculations. At the gate they tell you he has not been with them long – he was a circus bear and all his life he had been kept in a cage about two yards square

155

— you have been filming on location in Tunisia; you share a car back to Tunis with a Tunisian woman who was an extra in the film, and talk about the position of women in her country; she assures you that some do lead very restricted lives, yes, but many, like herself, have jobs and are as emancipated as any English woman. She has taken a perfume atomiser out of her bag as she talks, to refresh herself. Suddenly she turns it on you and squirts you several times. It is very friendly in intention but shocking, somehow primitive, doggy

— you are working in Italy again, doing *Façade*, but this time with a ballet company — a dance version; everyone is assembled in the wings in fair chaos for a first runthrough on the stage; at last the curtain goes up to discover, seated in the lotus position facing the auditorium, with his back to us, one of the dancers dressed only in a very short T-shirt.

307 I FOUND YET ANOTHER WAY to walk to the theatre, past the marzipan shop and through the pigeons in the Piazza in front of the Cathedral, and discovered that Milanese drivers don't know the meaning of the word pedestrian; and that Milanese dogs don't know the meaning of the word lamp-post.

On the other hand, walking along in this city people meet your eye, men and women; and with interest, not hostility.

308 IS IT ITALY OR THIS COMPANY? You can always rely on rehearsals being at least an hour late. The difficulty is to

know whether to be righteous, punctual, and demoralised, or righteous, late, and have an extra hour doing your own exhausting thing.

309 MILANESE PARKING REACHED ITS APOGEE FOR ME when the tram-driver stopped, rose from his seat and called upon one of the passengers to descend and guide the tram past a parked car that his tram was in danger of crushing. No good. So half the male passengers got out and shifted the car bodily to one side to make room. The first man guided the tram past and we glided on past the majestic gloomy columns of the Porta Ticinese. I don't know how often this happens but in his place I should have been tempted to shear off the side of the car. Clearly the Milanese aren't vindictive.

310 AT THE TRAM-STOP A WELL DRESSED YOUNG MAN, bearded, approached me and patiently, doggedly, asked me for coins to buy a *pannina*. He did this in three languages until finally the tram came, when his patience did snap a little at last. I suffered merely the discomfiture of the slumbering bourgeoise, at being made to face something; and puzzled – because of his clothes – as to exactly what.

Inside the tram, a more universal shock at the sight of the man who clambered on and was lurched, as the car jerked on, almost into the lap of one of the passengers. One side of his face was greatly disfigured, the left eyelid drooping out and red, as the eye was, weeping (his other eye was small and blue). The skin stretched on that side of his face, with seams, and the lower lip turned almost inside out. It looked, but not quite, as if he had been badly burned; and then he took out, scrabbling to open and read, a folded shiny leaflet, with hands like claws, skin stretched again over deformed bones, bent like arthritis, but not swollen. It was hard to tell if all the fingers were there. He seemed alright with himself, used to himself; he spoke to the man he bumped into but did not hang on an answer. He was an object of fascination and horror for the other passengers – did he always carry a leaflet to study? He got off at the May 14th Piazza and stood for a long time waiting by the side of the tram.

311 IT WAS A TERRIBLE MISTAKE not to bring lots to read. I should never have listened to John, who expected me to spend my spare time walking around Milan and soaking up the *genius loci*. I have already finished the Angela Carter essays and the Forster and I am being lazy about newspapers. I don't know Italian well enough to read more than the Photoromances, which I do enjoy, or to understand the radio. By the time I get home at night I am desperate to hear or read other voices. It was a great comfort to speak to Virginia in Florence. She says she will send me a few books. She is full of Bach and told me that I must listen to the recording Glenn Gould made of the Goldberg Variations before he died – she knew I had been given his first recording, made after he had given up live concerts and would only make records, I don't much like the version I have because it is so cold. I like Bach played the way people expect Chopin to be played, and vice versa.

312

things you did do

– you are working with a ballet company in Milan, doing a version of *Façade*. You have complained all week to the management about people taking photographs during the performance, frequently with flashlights, and the interruptions have died down; but one afternoon you are in mid-beat, counting furiously for when to come in again, when a woman in the front row stands up with her camera to immortalise the scene. Very thrown, you limp to the end of the piece as best you can, but backstage swear that you will not go on again until she or her camera or both are removed. Everyone flaps about uselessly and your next cue approaches. You feel that honour is at stake – you should make a stand. Courage fails you. You go on. But as the orchestra strikes up (they are situated on the stage behind you so that of course you can never see the conductor ...) you find yourself waving your hand at them as if polishing a mirror, and hear your voice in a passable if shrill impersonation of Anna Magnani, saying, '*Scusi! Scusi!*' Then you turn towards the woman, your hand now palm uppermost in the 'alms for Allah' gesture: '*Ma!? ... Ma non posso continuare con questo ...* ' (What is the word for camera? You indicate the apparatus eloquently.) The lady curls up in her seat like a wood-louse. The orchestra strikes up again, the show goes on.

Some of your colleagues give you the thumbs up, some of them look coldly because of your unprofessional conduct. When you come off, the charming lighting-man, Nuccio, who has promised one day to make you some of his famous spaghetti napoletana, chides you gently, 'You know, Eleonora, you really *should* take hashish – then these little things would not bother you!'

313 THE BLACK SWANS AT LEEDS CASTLE are so spoiled that they glide up to you shamelessly, requiring food. We had nothing with us to give them but I had watched them a few

moments before elegantly sifting weeds from the water, so I offered them tufts of grass that I pulled up beside the steps. Still I was surprised that they accepted so greedily and lingered for more. Raw vegetables – probably better for them than biscuits or stale crusts. Or perhaps it's just that food always tastes better if you haven't prepared it yourself.

314   *things that make you think that some things*
are worth the effort and/or suffering

– the hedges that have been clipped to spell out the name of TOPSHAM railway station, and the daffodils you can see from the train on a grassy bank outside Swindon, that spell out SPRING IS SPRUNG

– a man in a small London restaurant, who clearly doubts very much whether he ought to disturb you and your companion, but feels compelled finally to come over to your table, ask permission to introduce himself – a very infrequent theatregoer who remembered a performance of yours he saw ten years ago, and wanted to thank you

315   I FELT RATHER ELDERLY and extremely foolish and it took quite a lot of determination to force myself back for the afternoon session of the 'Shared Experience' workshop but I am glad that I did. I might not have made much of a stab at being 'a gusty flurry on the blasted heath', but I reckon my 'underground torrent', writhing and bashing my way past all the other, as yet unawakened, torrents littering the floor of the church hall, was something quite startling in the way of interpretation.

160

316 THERE WAS AN AWFUL LOT OF COMMITMENT at the American-style 'performance weekend' I went to; but I suspect that was because the fee was so high. To pay out that much money you must feel a strong need, so you start off with a lot of psyche as well as cash at stake. It was interesting, certainly. About forty people congregating to get to know each other and themselves, with a view to rediscovering their direction, confidence, joy in performance and the ability to take risks and criticism. Seductive promises, with a slight touch of the panacea about them. All we had to do was to pay the money and prepare a two-minute performance of any kind, recite, act, sing, dance, play an instrument. It was not exactly a lost weekend — fascinating to watch a group of total strangers transform themselves over fifty-six hours into familiars and cronies, if not intimates. But it had nothing to do with performance.

The sessions were peppered with techniques taken variously from the schools of behavioural science, family therapy and brainwashing, and I suppose in fact it was a kind of mild encounter therapy. They disjoint all your normal timing so that you lose your bearings, eating at odd unanticipatable times, staying up hours past your bed-time, and sleeping very little. Fear (of exposure and of the looming two-minute performance), sleeplessness and lofty stakes, plus the prevailing atmosphere of love and approval (just occasionally laced with bracing disapproval in selected cases) combine to produce a sense of being high and together and achieving the impossible. But though the tutor was astute and gifted, the actual work done was not impressive. Now and then a word or a hint enabled a performer to move forward or to step out of his own hide and be something else or more, but this was exceptional, and too often bad or garish work was applauded and passed over. It felt like a prolonged therapy session or even a religious revival, rather than a craft work-

161

shop; and even in this context the shouts of encouragement and approval from the 'back row' of inanely grinning initiates seemed excessive and misleading. In a sense what they are offering is the experience of perfect childhood – love flowing like milk and honey – in case you missed out on that and are screwed up therefore. And this is not compatible, for professional actors, with maintaining critical standards.

317 WE DO SEEM TO BE GOING THE AMERICAN WAY: there are more and more professional workshops, classes, workouts – Shakespeare, Stanislavsky, improvisation, tap-dancing, movement, stillness . . . Whether this is because work is scarcer and actors more than ever numerous, and despair – and the need to keep limber your fugitive skills – is stronger, I don't know. The situation in America always had an element of the driven about it, a degree of panic behind the gargantuan enthusiasm. It was the terrible intensity of it all, in New York – the feeling that you had to be an actor, nothing but an actor, twenty-five hours a day, seen in the right places and forever limbering – that drove me back to England in the days when New York was 'wide open'. It seemed to me then, that here actors have lives and homes and interests outside acting; they are more like real people, and that seems a good and even a useful thing for an actor. But certainly most American actors can teach us a lot about dedication and commitment.

It strikes me that over the longer term all the things that were promised at that weekend – the return of 'joy', confidence, daring, and more besides – come out of attending ordinary professional classes and workshops as I have been, at the Actors' Centre and with 'Shared Experience' and elsewhere, especially interesting to me because I never went to

Drama School. You do start overcoming fears and foibles — or at least learning to pin-point them for yourself, and that's a beginning. So I am grateful for the American influence and the opportunities now abounding. I just hope that all the work done in class does not have to remain in limbo. Even the leaderless classes we conducted ourselves, contending with all the excellent problems of the democratic process, were full of illuminations and insights that come just from watching other people struggling, with nerves, or with a piece of text. And nothing is more exhilarating, in workshop — or rehearsal for that matter — than having a director, a tutor, or another actor, who takes a piece of text or of behaviour and opens doors and lets in light that makes everyone hilarious, with that delight that comes almost always not from finding out something new, but from a shock of recognition, of being reminded of something so obvious that you knew it, somewhere, all the time. If you can offer something back, and something back, and yet again, and on and on — wonderful!

318 WELL — WHEN I DID PLAY CLEOPATRA I wore a dress — gold lamé with Egyptian pleating. I did not bare my breasts but the bodice was cut sparely and plunged very deep. One man in the audience watched the performance in total absorption, riveted. When I fell to my knees and bowed low before Octavius Caesar he turned to his neighbour and said, 'There! I told you they wouldn't fall out!'

319   *things that make you feel that there is one*
                        law for you and another for everyone else

— your mother, unable to get seats for a play she wants to see, telephones the theatre a second time, asks for the

163

Manager and says that she is you. You are astonished to hear that he was delighted to let her/you have two House seats. You decide to try it yourself next time

320 WE WERE TALKING ABOUT POSTERITY and what we would like to have lent our names to in a future world. Jean said that she had always wanted to have a rose named after her — and of course now there is one so she is happy. Greta decided she would like it to be a cocktail and June a wrestling hold. I had always thought that it would be nice to give my name to a hat, or even just a style of hat, or a way of wearing it, as people say 'a Garbo hat'; but I remembered that in my dressing-room in Milan there was 'Garbo ' lavatory paper in the lavatory, with a lady peeping out through greenery, and the description *è morbidezza naturale* ... Perhaps oblivion is best.

321 YESTERDAY IN THE QUEUE at the wine and spirits counter at Littlewoods there were two people in front of me. The first, a man, was wearing a dark duffle-coat and a little hat of navy wool. His hair was dark and his face was almost obscured by a black beard. While he was waiting for the assistant to bring him his bottle he turned to the woman behind him and spoke, in a confidential tone, with a slightly transatlantic accent, 'If you look around, you can see not just one but two movie stars here in this store,' he said.

She made a noise of polite surprise.

'Yes,' he went on, 'that woman behind you is a movie star. She was in *Help!*, the Beatles film. Her name is Fenella Fielding.'

During his next revelation I was busying myself with my basket.

164

'You probably didn't see my film, *The Alamo*. That was a year or two ago.'

He paid for his bottle and slid it into his pocket saying, half to himself and half at large as he moved away, 'It really is great to bother *other people* for a change!'

322   *things that show which way the last straw is blowing*

— you have been out of work for several months and the horizon is empty; then out of the blue a script is delivered by taxi from the B.B.C. With high hopes you open the envelope and glance at the covering letter. Before you start to read the script you riffle through the pages to see when the character named by the director's secretary makes her first appearance. By now you are used to reading about 'Mrs X — a handsome woman in her late thirties to mid-forties' or 'Y — no longer in her first youth but still attractive'. The stage direction here says simply, 'A middle-aged woman pushes her way forward ... '

323 WHY IS IT ALWAYS SUCH A THRILL TO SEE hot-air balloons? Is it because I used to associate them with stories like Babar, or old photographs, and think of them as something from the past; so that now, although you see them more and more often, they always seem like history? Or is it because of their silence? And stateliness? When I went to meet a friend at Temple Meads station I counted thirteen balloons crossing the horizon, yellow, red, blue, rainbow — an invasion (or an escape) of balloons. And once, between Newbury and Andover, driving towards the sunset, there was a huge red balloon rising above the pine trees, incredibly close, and it floated away like a dream.

— Fellini telephones and says how sorry he is that he did not get to meet you, it was a terrible error and the person responsible has been sacked; he wants you to work with him in a film with Marlon Brando, Oskar Werner, Gerard Depardieu, Leo McKern, Ian Charleson, Robert de Niro, Sylvia Coleridge, Allida Valli, Katherine Hepburn and Candice Bergen and asks for any suggestions you may have about casting

— you start having singing lessons again and develop a magnificent contralto voice and become an opera singer

— you become any kind of singer with the voice you have

— you stop apologising

— you hear that a play you have always wanted to be in is being given a splendid production on television; you feel sadly sure that the casting of your part must have been simultaneous with the decision to do the play, but you alert your agent anyway; to your surprise the producer and director agree to see you; they are charming and full of praise for your work on television; they talk about the play, not much about the part and look forward to seeing you after Christmas when rehearsals start. After you have got over the shock, you decide to dedicate your life to setting up a new Award: for imaginative casting

— after two cancellations, because of a strike, you finally get beyond rehearsing and actually record the play you have always wanted to do; and for once — something so rare, especially in television, where time presses and fear curdles and the studio so often deforms what was beginning to take shape in the rehearsal room – you feel that it really has happened. For once all the elements marry; the acting, on the whole, goes well (as far as it is ever possible to judge) and the sets, the costumes, the lighting, the camerawork are so good – there is a wonderful atmosphere in the studio, of good humour and concentration. Afterwards there are drinks in the production office, instead of the desperate, divisive, smoke-filled B.B.C. Club, so you are all together and each department full of admiration for what each other department was able to realise, and delight, and a sense that we have all been working on the same production; for once, something whole

– fantasy is not dead

326 ON A DAY WHEN IT WAS REALLY TOO HOT and muggy to move I forced myself to the Park for a walk and to see whether the herbaceous border on the Spanish Walk is as beautiful this year as last. Sadly it has been affected by the great heat, even after the deluges, and this year it only exists in patches, not as a whole. I went on past the wolves behind their wire and watched their sinister panting and loping and turning, and one of them immobile, listening. I decided to go in and went straight to the rhinoceroses. Two were lying in the dust asleep. One sunk deep, literally in a hollow; one twitching its ears, and less oblivious. Little flurries of sand blew out from the ground in front of its nostrils. It shifted and twitched its ears and finally looked up and lumbered to its feet and ambled across to its partner and stuck its nose in the other one's rump. The other budged a little but did not rise. They stayed there nose to rump and were still so when I left.

Biography and Memoirs
also available in Methuen Paperbacks

Captain Robert Falcon Scott
SCOTT'S LAST EXPEDITION

Ernest Shepard
DRAWN FROM MEMORY / DRAWN FROM LIFE

Edith Templeton
THE SURPRISE OF CREMONA

Norman Thelwell
A MILLSTONE ROUND MY NECK
A PLANK BRIDGE BY A POOL

Tomi Ungerer
FAR OUT ISN'T FAR ENOUGH

Vivienne de Watteville
SPEAK TO THE EARTH